# Rice & Curry

# The Hippocrene International Cookbook Library

Afghan Food & Cookery

Alps, Cuisines of the

Aprovecho: A Mexican-American Border Cookbook

Argentina Cooks!, Exp. Ed.

Belarusian Cookbook, The

Bolivian Kitchen, My Mother's

Brazil: A Culinary Journey

Cajun Cuisine, Stir the Pot: The History of

Cajun Women, Cooking with

Calabria, Cucina di

Chile, Tasting

China's Fujian Province, Cooking from

Colombian Cooking, Secrets of

Corsican Cuisine

Croatian Cooking, Best of, Exp. Ed.

Czech Cooking, Best of, Exp. Ed.

Danish Cooking and Baking Traditions

Danube, All Along The, Exp. Ed.

Emilia-Romagna, The Cooking of

Egyptian Cuisine and Culture, Nile Style:

English Country Kitchen, The

Estonian Tastes and Traditions

Filipino Food, Fine

Finnish Cooking, Best of

Germany, Spoonfuls of

Greek Cooking, Regional

Haiti, Taste of

Havana Cookbook, Old (Bilingual)

Hungarian Cookbook, Exp. Ed.

India, A Culinary Journey

India, Flavorful

International Dictionary of Gastronomy

Jewish-Iraqi Cuisine, Mama Nazima's

Kerala Kitchen, The

Laotian Cooking, Simple

Lebanese Cookbook, The

Ligurian Kitchen, A

Lithuanian Cooking, Art of

Malaysia, Flavors of

Middle Eastern Kitchen, The

Naples, My Love for

Nepal, Taste of

New Hampshire: from Farm to Kitchen

New Jersey Cookbook, Farms and Foods of the Garden State:

Ohio, Farms and Foods of

Persian Cooking, Art of

Pied Noir Cookbook: French Sephardic Cuisine

Piemontese, Cucina: Cooking from Italy's Piedmont

Polish Cooking, Best of, Exp. Ed.

Polish Heritage Cookery, Ill. Ed.

Polish Holiday Cookery

Polish Traditions, Old

Portuguese Encounters, Cuisines of

Punjab, Menus and Memories from

Romania, Taste of

Russian Cooking, The Best of

Scottish-Irish Pub and Hearth Cookbook

Sephardic Israeli Cuisine

Sicilian Feasts

Slovenia, Flavors of

South Indian Cooking, Healthy

Spain, La Buena Mesa: The Regional Cooking of

Trinidad and Tobago, Sweet Hands: Island Cooking from

Turkish Cuisine, Taste of

Tuscan Kitchen, Tastes from a

Ukrainian Cuisine, Best of, Exp. Ed.

Uzbek Cooking, Art of

# Rice & Curry

## Sri Lankan Home Cooking

**S.H. Fernando Jr.**

**Photos by Susan Now**

HIPPOCRENE BOOKS

NEW YORK

Color photography by Susan Now.

Book and jacket design by Bryan Canniff.

For more information, address:
HIPPOCRENE BOOKS, INC.
171 Madison Avenue
New York, NY 10016
www.hippocrenebooks.com

Library of Congress Cataloging-in-Publication Data

Fernando, S. H.
  Rice & curry : Sri Lankan home cooking / S. H. Fernando
Jr. ; photos by Susan Now.
      p. cm.
  Includes index.
  ISBN-13: 978-0-7818-1273-3 (pbk.)
  ISBN-10: 0-7818-1273-9 (pbk.)
  1. Cooking, Sri Lankan. 2. Cookbooks.  I. Title. II. Title:
Rice and curry.
  TX724.5.S72F47 2011
  641.595493--dc23
                              2011025585

Printed in the United States of America.

*For Ammi*

# *Acknowledgments*

Thanks to all of those who aided and inspired me on this journey—especially my mother, Chandra Fernando, who raised me single-handedly with a lot of patience, love, and all of this incredible food. Thanks also to Uncle Cyril, Sid & Cynth, Siromi & Alain, and the rest of my family in Sri Lanka for their support, especially all of my wonderful aunts—Dora, Padma, Sita, Nalini, and Lalitha—and uncles and cousins (especially Sam and Sharmini). Thanks to Leela, Iraesha, Mihiri, Aunty Manel & Uncle Daya, Susan Now, Scotty Hard, Ramin Ganeshram, Kamini Mukunthan, Chef Koluu, Chef Ralph at The Mount Lavinia Hotel, Mr. O. Ivan P. de Silva and Chef Ananda Nihal at The Sitar Ltd., and Chenaka De Silva at Sigiri Restaurant, New York. Also thanks to Priti Gress and the entire staff at Hippocrene Books. ✤

# CONTENTS

# Foreword

Food has always intrigued and delighted me. One of my most vivid memories as a child, in fact, is climbing up on the kitchen counters to search the cupboards for cookies or other goodies, and stumbling upon an endless assortment of jars containing my mother's spices. This was my first introduction to cinnamon, coriander, cumin, nutmeg, cardamom, cloves, paprika, cayenne pepper powder, saffron, and much, much more. These spices seemed almost magical to me because I knew they were the secret ingredients my mother used to make our food taste so good. I remember curiously sniffing at the contents, poking a stubby finger in, dabbing a little on my tongue, and reveling in the different colors, flavors, smells, and textures. The moment of awakening for my taste buds had arrived.

Like any child, my undeveloped palate veered towards Chef-Boyardee, Swanson, or McDonald's, but not because I didn't like my mother's cooking. A native of Sri Lanka, she prepared a pot of fluffy basmati rice and various meat and vegetable curries a couple of times a week—the food that stands out most in my mind. Sometimes I would watch her in the kitchen as she used a medieval-looking grater to scrape the succulent white "meat" out of a freshly split coconut, or as she ground spices together with a traditional stone mortar and pestle. Never measuring ingredients, she would simply add a pinch of this or a sprinkle of that over some chicken, fish, or vegetables to create a delectable dish whose enticing aroma wafted through our entire apartment. I always remember she would close our bedroom doors so the curry smell didn't permeate the bed sheets and clothes hanging in the closets as well. To the tongue, the flavors were always pungent and distinct—incomparable to any pot roast or meatloaf I ate at friends' houses. Growing up on this deliciously different fare, it is hardly surprising that my tastes expanded to encompass other exotic flavors. Today my favorites include Vietnamese, Mexican, Malaysian, Indian, Middle Eastern, and Ethiopian food, but still, nothing I have ever had quite compares to my mother's rice and curry.

In college, I appreciated Sri Lankan food even more, being forced to suffer under mediocre institutional cooking for four years. Luckily, I could sometimes escape to my older brother's place, where by this time he was beginning to master the art of Sri Lankan home cooking. As the torch is inevitably handed down, so too did I acquire these skills over time. I discovered that not only was it infinitely easier than I had ever expected to prepare a curry, but this food also provided me with a crucial link to my culture.

In *Rice & Curry: Sri Lankan Home Cooking*, I dive headfirst into a rich culture and cuisine that is, in fact, one of the last culinary secrets of our time. As I conducted preliminary research online and at bookstores and libraries, I noticed that the food of practically every nation in the world is represented except Sri Lanka's. This is understandable considering this tiny island nation of some 20 million inhabitants could fit comfortably within the borders of New York State. Sri Lankan cuisine has also been sitting in the shadows of Indian food for some time. But things are quietly changing. A new breed of consumers fed on a steady diet of Food Network, the Travel Channel, and the Internet are expanding their horizons when it comes to food, and trying out new things in the kitchen. Authentic restaurants are opening in ethnic enclaves like Staten Island, New York, which boasts one of the largest communities of Sri Lankans living in the U.S. Also, ingredients like coconut milk, lemongrass, even curry leaves are more widely available at national outlets like Whole

Foods. The world is generally getting smaller, and Sri Lanka, already internationally known in the sport of cricket, is ready to reveal her sensational tastes. With its ease of preparation, substantial dietary benefits (from the use of Ayurvedic herbs) and pure flavor, Sri Lankan cooking is poised to make a dramatic splash on the culinary horizon.

When I set out on this journey a lot of people asked me, "Why you? You're not a chef!" But I take pride in the fact that cooking is not a job for me, but an adventure, and something done out of love. As a journalist, I also believe that any scribe worth his words should know his subject inside and out. So in order to really understand and master the art of Sri Lankan cooking, I spent a year there, and learned from the ground up—

from the numerous spices used to the actual recipes themselves. I cooked practically every day, perfecting the dishes included in these pages, and testing them out on members of my large extended family in Sri Lanka. My aunts, uncles, cousins, and friends, in fact, are responsible for providing many of these recipes. Which helps to illustrate another point: Rice and curry is folk cooking, prepared and eaten every day at home. The complexity of flavors masks the ease of preparation. While you may be intimidated at first by strange ingredients and the complete novelty of it all, the best way of learning is by doing. The tantalizing photos will let you know what to expect for your toils, and by using the Sample Menus (page 202) to put together a typical Sri Lankan table, you are in for a real taste of paradise. ✤

# Introduction

It speaks to the creativity and imagination of a people that by utilizing the natural bounty around them—the seeds, nuts, fruits, roots, leaves, and bark of plants and trees—they could create a cuisine as pleasing to the palate as it is healthy for mind and body and satisfying to the soul. Popularly known as 'rice and curry,' the national cuisine of Sri Lanka actually comprises a variety of preparations, from pungent to pacifying, served together and mixed and eaten with the fingers to create a complex tapestry of sights, smells, flavors, and textures. Whereas a typical western menu is meted out in courses, one after another, a rice and curry meal involves a glorious medley of dishes served simultaneously—including at least one meat or seafood main dish, several vegetables, plenty of rice, a fresh salad, and a sweet chutney or sour pickle—thereby covering the whole spectrum of flavors.

The key to rice and curry is in the infinite combinations and, of course, exactly the right proportions when it comes to spicing. For curry itself is not a single spice but a very sophisticated blend of coriander, cumin, cinnamon, cardamom, clove, fenugreek, black pepper, mustard seeds, and the indispensable curry leaf. All of these spices have applications in the ancient Ayurvedic system of holistic health, and were probably used just as much for their digestive and preservative properties as for flavor enhancement—especially in the days before refrigeration. There are also as many recipes for curry as there are cooks making it, and chili powder or cayenne pepper powder, despite popular notions to the contrary, is not an ingredient of curry powder (except in Jaffna curry powder), though it is inevitably added to dishes in the cooking process. Sri Lankans, in fact, tend to lace their curries with major doses of chili powder (known in the west as cayenne pepper powder)—the fiery nature of their food is one of the hallmarks of this cuisine and one that distinguishes it from tamer North Indian fare,

to which it is often compared. Another major difference in the cuisines of these two Asian neighbors lies in Indian food's reliance on dairy such as milk, ghee (clarified butter), and yogurt, while Sri Lankans naturally favor coconut oil and coconut milk owing to the surplus of palm trees that cover the island. The addition of animal fat makes Indian food much heavier in comparison, though not necessarily tastier, because coconut, too, contains its own flavor-enhancing fat—and one that researchers are now discovering contains many beneficial properties.

Just as curry is not a single spice, so too are there a variety of curries. Red curries are usually the hottest, deriving their name from the large amount of chili powder used. Black curries require a roasting of spices (as well as the addition of shredded coconut and raw rice grains) prior to use, releasing added flavor, while in brown curries, these same spices are used unroasted, most often in the preparation of vegetables. Finally, white curries, which are actually yellow-tinged from the addition of turmeric, derive their name from their main ingredient, coconut milk, and are usually the mildest in taste.

In preparing curries, a good curry powder is only part of the equation. Seasoning food is often a three step process that involves marinating (especially meat dishes), slow cooking, and finally "tempering," a practice essential to Sri Lankan cooking. This process involves frying onions, curry leaves, and sometimes mustard seeds or even curry powder in oil or ghee and adding this to the completed dish prior to serving. Tempering is especially helpful for boosting the flavor of a dish that has been frozen or cooked a couple of days in advance.

To the casual observer, the preparation of Sri Lankan food may seem complex and time consuming. Of course, in the traditional Sri Lankan kitchen, usually located at the back of a house and equipped with an open hearth, clay pots, and

*A street vendor's cart*

such utensils as a mortar and pestle or grinding stone used to powder spices, it probably was. But the purpose of this book is to take away the mystery and show that what seems difficult is rather very doable. In our modern era of food processors and coffee grinders and readily available ingredients like canned coconut milk, much of the preparation time has been cut in half.

Once you have made a batch of curry powder, for example, by roasting and grinding all the spices, this mixture will last for some months in a sealed glass jar in the fridge. Other ingredients, such as curry leaves or lemongrass, are best used fresh and not in their dried or powdered form. If you are concerned with truly authentic flavor, unrefined coconut oil is the oil of choice used in most of these recipes, but olive oil or any vegetable oil is a perfectly acceptable alternative. Sri Lankans also tend to use Bombay or red onions, which lack the sweetness of their white and yellow cousins popular in the west, but either kind is acceptable. Finally, while ingredients like pandanus (rampe), gamboge (goraka) and Maldive fish

may be hard to find in the west, it is well worth a look for them in the quest for authentic flavor.

Speaking of authenticity, all of the recipes in this book come from regular people like you and me. After all, Sri Lankan food is folk cooking best prepared at home. While I have enjoyed plenty of meals at fancy restaurants and little roadside "hotels" that are popular for Sri Lankan fast food, the best food I have eaten was at peoples' homes. Sri Lankan cooks are famous for not measuring ingredients, but rather adding a dash of this or a handful of that. My task was to take their approximations and experiment and adapt until I was able to sufficiently reproduce what can only be described as "that authentic taste." Unlike cookbooks that offer flawed recipes that never turn out correctly—some by well-known chefs—all of the recipes in this book have been tried, tested, and tasted by yours truly and many members of my family in Sri Lanka. If I can make these dishes, so can you,

Happy cooking and good eating! ✤

# A Brief History of the Resplendent Isle

Situated in the Indian Ocean, a pearl-shaped drop just off the southernmost tip of India, Sri Lanka has been known since antiquity by such names as Serendib, The Resplendent Isle, Isle of Delight, Isle of Gems, or simply Taprobane (meaning "paradise" in ancient Greek). While evidence of primitive human life there can be traced back some 1,750,000 years ago (to ancestors of the island's aboriginal people or Veddahs), the first major literary and historical reference to the island appears in the great Hindu epic, *The Ramayana* (circa 500 BCE). This story tells of the god Rama's conquest of Lanka, as it was then called, in 3000 BCE after Lanka's demon king, Ravana, abducts Sita, his wife. Rama sends the monkey god Hanuman to retrieve her, and he succeeds, supposedly burning down the island in the process.

Myth and legend further meld with historical fact in *The Mahavamsa* ("Great Genealogy"), a Sri Lankan text compiled in the ancient Pali language in the sixth century BCE, in which King Vijaya, the grandson of a kidnapped Indian princess and an amorous lion, Sinha, becomes the first ruler of the Sinhalese people. From both accounts, we get an impression of a beautiful island rich in natural resources and already host to a well-developed civilization five hundred years before Christ. In fact, Buddhism came to Sri Lanka very early on, in 306 BCE, and it was here that the oral teachings of the Buddha, known as the *Tripitaka*, were first committed to writing and soon adopted by royalty and the masses alike.

While most of the island's early history played out as a power struggle between Aryan kings (descended from northern India) and Dravidian invaders (from southern India), the character of Sri Lanka changed drastically with the arrival of the European colonial powers—beginning with the Portuguese in the sixteenth century (1505-1658), and continuing

with the Dutch (1640-1796), and finally the British (1796-1948). Not coincidentally, western interest in the tiny island had a lot to do with the robust trade in spices, especially cinnamon, which was a precious commodity traded with Egypt as far back as 1400 BCE. In addition to introducing Christianity into this predominantly Buddhist country, the Europeans brought with them their own languages, customs, and cultural biases, which left an indelible impression on the natives. The Europeans also left an infrastructure and institutions (such as the parliamentary form of government) that have lasted into the present century.

Sri Lanka finally gained its independence from the British in 1948. Today, despite having one of the lowest per capita incomes, it boasts one of the highest standards of living in all of Southeast Asia, as well as

a 90 percent literacy rate (while the official languages are Sinhalese and Tamil, English is still prevalent in urban areas of the country). It ranks third behind only India and China in the production of tea, and exports rubber as well as crops such as rice, coconuts, and not surprisingly, spices (cinnamon, cardamom, cloves, nutmeg). Brilliant gemstones—blue sapphires, star sapphires, cats' eyes, and moonstones—are another of Sri Lanka's natural treasures.

Of its 20 million inhabitants, Buddhist Sinhalese comprise a majority of 74 percent, the largely Hindu Tamils, 13 percent, Muslims (descended from Arab merchants and Malay workers imported by the Dutch), 7 percent, and Christian Burghers (the mixed-race descendents of Europeans) round out a multi-ethnic, multi-religious society. This diverse populace has largely lived together in peace until simmering Tamil-Sinhala tensions sparked riots in 1983 that lead to conflict, unrest, and a 30-year struggle which was only resolved in May 2009 with the defeat of the Tamil Tiger terrorist group.

With the war now a page from the past, Sri Lanka may be appreciated once again as a resplendent island of dramatic sunsets and golden beaches, lush jungles and towering highlands, green paddy fields and tea plantations, a friendly and humble populace, and a cuisine that is one of the world's best-kept secrets. For unless you have been to a Sri Lankan expat's home or visited the island itself, chances are you have not tasted the fiery, coconut milk-infused curries and all their delectable accompaniments. Sri Lankan food or 'rice and curry' as it is more commonly known, is a meal best enjoyed at home, with the hands, and in the company of friends and family. ❖

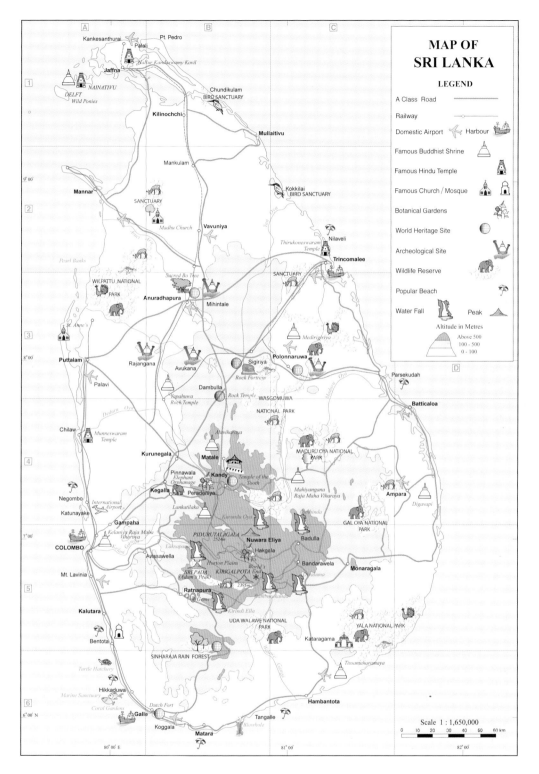

# MAP OF SRI LANKA

## LEGEND

A Class Road

Railway

Domestic Airport / Harbour

Famous Buddhist Shrine

Famous Hindu Temple

Famous Church / Mosque

Botanical Gardens

World Heritage Site

Archeological Site

Wildlife Reserve

Popular Beach

Water Fall / Peak

Altitude in Metres
Above 500
100 - 500
0 - 100

Kankesanthurai
Pt. Pedro
Palali
Jaffna
Nallur Kandaswamy Kovil
NAINATIVU
DELFT
Wild Ponies
Chundikulam
BIRD SANCTUARY
Kilinochchi
Mullaitivu
Mankulam
Kokkilai
BIRD SANCTUARY
Mannar
SANCTUARY
Vavuniya
Madhu Church
Thirukoneswaram
Temple
Nilaveli
Trincomalee
Pearl Banks
Sacred Bo Tree
SANCTUARY
WILPATTU NATIONAL
PARK
Anuradhapura
Mihintale
St. Anne's
Puttalam
Palavi
Rajangana
Avukana
Medirigiriya
Sigiriya
Polonnaruwa
Parsekudah
Yapahuwa
Rock Temple
Dambulla
Rock Temple
Rock Fortress
WASGOMUWA
NATIONAL PARK
Batticaloa
Chilaw
Munneswaram
Temple
Havihakosa
Kurunegala
Matale
MADURU OYA NATIONAL
PARK
Pinnawala
Elephant
Orphanage
Kandy
Temple of the
Tooth
Kegalla
Peradeniya
Mahiyangana
Raja Maha Viharaya
Ampara
Digavapi
Lankatilaka
Kurunchi Oya
GAL OYA NATIONAL
PARK
Negombo
International
Airport
Katunayake
Gampaha
Kelaniya Raja Maha
Viharaya
PIDURUTALAGALA
2524m
Nuwara Eliya
Badulla
COLOMBO
Avissawella
Hakgala
Hicton Plains
Bandarawela
Monaragala
Mt. Lavinia
Laksapana
SRI PADA
(Adam's Peak)
World's End
KIRIGALPOTA
2395m
Ratnapura
Gems
Kirindi Ella
Kalutara
UDA WALAWE NATIONAL
PARK
YALA NATIONAL PARK
Bentota
Katharagama
SINHARAJA RAIN FOREST
Tissamaharamaya
Turtle Hatchery
Hikkaduwa
Marine Sanctuary
Coral Gardens
Hambantota
Dutch Fort
Galle
Tangalle
Koggala
Matara

Scale 1 : 1,650,000
0  10  20  30  40  50  60 km

80°00' E
81°00'
82°00'

9°00'
8°00'
7°00'
6°00' N

A    B    C    D
1
2
3
4
5
6

*A Buddha statue in the southern town of Galle*

# Traveling to Sri Lanka:
# A Primer

So, you want to make Sri Lankan food at home. But do you know how this food is supposed to taste? Chances are that unless you are lucky enough to live in a city like New York with its sizeable Sri Lankan immigrant community (who have opened several authentic restaurants) or you personally know a Sri Lankan expat and have been invited to his/her house for dinner, the answer is probably, 'no.' So the next logical question is, 'How are you going to make food that you've never tasted?' The answer is quite simple: Jump on a plane to Sri Lanka, and find out for yourself!

In the wake of the end of hostilities in the 30-year conflict between the Sri Lankan government and the separatist terrorist group the Liberation Tigers of Tamil Eelam (LTTE) in May 2009, *The New York Times* declared this beautiful island nation one of the ten best tourist destinations of 2010. Since then, Sri Lanka has seen a steady and significant rise in tourism, which continues to grow. Sri Lanka might be halfway around the world, but it is well within your reach, and this chapter promises to break down some of the questions you might have about planning a trip to this island paradise.

## Essentials

- **Sri Lanka is 5.5 hours ahead** of Greenwich Mean Time (GMT + 5.5) and 11.5 hours ahead of Eastern Standard Time (EST) in the U.S. (EST + 11.5). Sri Lanka does not observe Daylight Savings Time.

- **Currency** is the Sri Lankan rupee; approximately US $1 = 115 rupees.

- **Voltage requirements:** 230/240 volts AC; 50 Hz. Round 2 or 3 pin plugs are the norm.

- **Credit cards** accepted in urban areas; ATMs and high-speed Internet service are also readily available here, but much less as you move outside the cities.

- **Cell phones:** If you are visiting for an extended stay, think about getting a local SIM card (SL Telecom or Dialog), for which you can pay to add minutes. Cell phone calls overseas are even cheaper than a call from a land line.

- **Tipping:** 10% service is added to hotel and restaurant bills, but anything additional is appreciated—especially for drivers/cabbies.

## When To Go

No time is a bad time to visit Sri Lanka, which lies roughly 373 miles north of the Equator and enjoys average yearly temperatures between 82 and 86 degrees Fahrenheit. But the official tourist season runs from December to April, allowing you to avoid the southwest monsoon season (between May and July) as well as the worst of the heat and humidity, which peaks in April. The shorter northeast monsoon season only runs from December to January, so it should only affect your trip if you are in that part of the country at that time.

The trishaw, a popular means of transport in Sri Lanka

## Getting There and Getting Around

These days there is no shortage of international carriers that fly to Sri Lanka. Emirates, Qatar, and Kuwait Airlines all offer flights from the U.S. that usually stop off in the Middle East, while Sri Lankan Airlines, Air India, Kingfisher, Lufthansa, KLM, and Swissair fly direct from major cities in Europe. Thai Airlines, Cathay Pacific, Malaysian, and Quantas are also options if you are flying from the west coast.

Once on the island, depending on your plans, there are a variety of ways to get around. First of all, a cab to downtown Colombo from one of Bandaranaike International Airport's taxi counters will run you between 1,500 and 2,000 rupees (about US $13 to $17). During your stay you may hire air-conditioned taxis (for 30 rupees per km), trishaws (or tuk-tuks), which will require some bargaining skills, or even a car and driver (for US $25/day). Buses can get you around a big city like Colombo for pennies, but you would need to inquire about specific routes. Trains are suitable for intercity travel, for example, the amazing three-hour climb from coastal Colombo to Kandy, the ancient kingdom in the hills.

## Where To Stay

Colombo boasts a nice variety of very affordable 5-star hotels, and beach resorts abound—especially in popular tourist areas like Hikkaduwa and Galle in the south. In addition to mainstays like the Intercontinental, The Hilton, and my personal favorite, the privately owned, colonial-era Galle Face Hotel, you may also elect to stay at the stylish Taj Sumudra or the luxurious Cinnamon Grand. Visit the official site of Sri Lankan tourism, *www.srilanka.travel,* for more suggestions and information on holiday homes, guesthouses, boutique hotels, econo-lodges, and luxury apartments for rent. In fact, this site will be essential in planning your trip.

## Safety

Since the end of hostilities in May 2009, Sri Lankan authorities have reported that not a single incident related to the war has disrupted the newly found peace on the island. While street crime and violent crime are negligible here, common sense suggests that you always keep an eye on your wallet, are mindful of your surroundings, and do not go off somewhere with strangers. There are also certain cardinal rules that apply in the tropics. Stay hydrated with plenty of bottled water, and never drink tap water. Also avoid ice and juices in places that seem to have questionable hygiene. Bring sunscreen because the close proximity to the Equator makes the sun much stronger here, and also be sure to use mosquito repellent to avoid being feasted upon. As an alternative to the DDT-based repellents, I usually bring some citronella oil, which does the job quite well. Those with sensitive stomachs, who are not accustomed to eating spicy food, might also want to bring an antacid or anti-diarrheal medicine, and refrain from eating street foods.

## Some important local numbers:

**Fire: 242 2222**
**Ambulance: 242 2222**
**Police: 243 3333**

## Health & Medical Facilities

If you do happen to fall sick in Sri Lanka, the good news is that excellent and very affordable medical and dental care is right on hand. During my year-long stay there, working on this book, I had occasion to go to the best private hospital in Colombo, Durden's, both for a couple of emergency room visits as well as a full physical. In the emergency room, a doctor saw me immediately, and gave me a prescription for antibiotics— the visit and the drugs costing only a few dollars each. My full physical, with blood work included, cost me a whopping US $35. I have since had dental work done in Sri Lanka—a crown, an extraction, and a filling—and all procedures combined cost me less than US $200. Though Sri Lanka is not as popular as India or Thailand for medical tourism, I'm sure it's going to earn a reputation for that soon.

## Points of Interest

For a tiny tropical island, Sri Lanka is brimming with enough attractions to satisfy anyone, from the most ardent adventurer to the laziest beach bum. Whether it is sports, shopping, sightseeing, or just soaking up some rays, the following list provides a brief rundown of what's worth checking out on the island.

### Sun & Surf

Relaxing or rollicking in the sun, surf, and sand is probably the number one reason many tourists visit Sri Lanka each year. In fact, going "down south," is local parlance for a vacation at one of Sri Lanka's picturesque beaches. Roughly two hours south of Colombo, **Bentota** and **Hikkaduwa** have long been home to many fine resorts. But venture another hour just past Galle (known for its well-preserved 17th-century Dutch fort) and you will find far less crowded beaches such as **Unawatuna**. Further along in the "deep south," which includes towns like **Weligama, Mirissa,** and **Tangalle**, you might even have a whole beach to yourself. Now that the conflict is over, think about heading to the pristine East coast, known for its white sand and blue waters. The first place worth stopping is the idyllic **Arugam Bay**, a haven for surfers and snorklers. Further up the east coast are the towns of **Batticaloa** and **Trincomalee,** whose natural harbor provides for a whole host of aquatic activities including dolphin watching. Now that the north is completely open, you can also check out some of the untouched beaches and lagoons around **Jaffna** and the northernmost town of **Point Pedro**.

*A stupa in the ancient city of Anuradhapura*

### Historical Sites

Sri Lanka is home to six UNESCO world heritage sites, four of which happen to be in the north central part of the island in an area called the 'Cultural Triangle.' These include the sacred city of Anuradhapura, the ancient capital of Polonnaruwa, the caves of Dambulla, and Sigiriya rock fortress. Located about 128 miles from Colombo, **Anuradhapura** was a major Buddhist center dating back to the 4th century BCE. In addition to numerous Buddha statues, the site is famous for its ancient irrigation tanks as well as the Sri Maha Bodhi, which was grown from the original tree under which the Buddha attained enlightenment. Built in the 12th century AD, **Polonnaruwa,** one of Sri Lanka's ancient capitals, is the home to many pyramid-like dagobas or stupas, which house Buddhist relics. Nearby stands the massive rock fortress of **Sigiriya** and the fantastically painted caves of **Dambulla.** Usually a three-day trip is sufficient to cover all these sites. The other UNESCO archaeological site, located due south in the city of Galle, is the 17th-century **Dutch Fort**, which has been recently restored to its former glory with the addition of several great boutique hotels. The ancient hill city of **Kandy**, another UNESCO site, is the seat of the last Sri Lankan kingdom as well as the site of the Dalada Maligawa or **Temple of The Tooth**, which houses the Buddha's tooth relic.

## Nature

Sri Lanka's natural beauty and wildlife are unmatched. From national parks to botanical gardens, travel in any direction outside the bustling capital of Colombo and find yourself in a new world of wonder. From the 7,358-foot peak of Sri Pada or **Adam's Peak,** located in the central highlands, to the **Pinnawela Elephant Orphanage,** a short drive from Kandy, fully immerse yourself in the countryside to truly appreciate Sri Lanka's true untouched splendor. As far as national parks go, **Yala** in the south and **Kaudulla** in the northeast are supposed to support the greatest number of animals, including herds of elephants, sloth bears, and leopards. Or you could opt for a walk through the **Royal Botanical Gardens** of Peradeniya (outside Kandy). A visit to the numerous tea estates outside of Kandy and Nuwara Eliya, in the central highlands, also provides a delightful hill country excursion, and a chance to sample the finest teas at their source.

**Temple of The Tooth in Kandy**

## Eco-Tourism

Tourism to regions of ecological interest has grown exponentially in the last several years, and true nature lovers visiting Sri Lanka should not miss two sites in particular—the **Sinharaja Rainforest Reserve**, a UNESCO World Heritage site located in the southwest of the island, and **Knuckles Conservation Forest**, located near the central highlands. For further information, please consult two websites specifically designed to answer further questions on eco-tourism in Sri Lanka:

**The Sri Lanka Eco Tourism Foundation**
*www.ecotourismsrilanka.net*

**Eco Team Sri Lanka** *www.srilankaecotourism.com*

## Public Holidays & Festivals

*Poya* – Each month's full moon day is commemorated by a Buddhist public holiday in Sri Lanka with banks and offices closed, and meat and alcohol unavailable for purchase (outside of hotels where most foreigners stay). The Vesak Poya in May is especially significant, marking Lord Buddha's birth, enlightenment, and death, and is celebrated by a festival of lights in which people make all manner of lanterns.

*Esala Perahera* – A huge nighttime procession of elephants, dancers, drummers, fire-eaters, and acrobats marks this popular Kandy festival in which the sacred Buddha tooth relic is brought out of its home in the Dalada Maligawa Temple.

*Thai Ponggal* – A Tamil harvest festival that occurs in mid-January.

*Maha Sivarathi (Great Night of Shiva)* – A Tamil festival honoring Lord Shiva that occurs around February/March.

*Deepavali* – Also known as Diwali or the Festival of Lights, this is one of the bigger Hindu festivals. The date is dependent on the lunar/solar Hindu calendar, but usually occurs around October/November.

*Galle Literary Festival* – The

*Wild elephants at the Pinnawela elephant orphanage*

Island's premier literary event, featuring authors from home and abroad that occurs at the end of January.
***Hikkaduwa Beach Festival*** – A more recent, four-day beach festival featuring food, fun, and international deejays that occurs at the end of July.

## Shopping

Colombo is a shopper's delight for those in search of unique finds, bargains, and just the right souvenir of their trip. Whether it be precious gemstones, beautiful batiks and textiles, or some premium Ceylon tea, there is certainly something for everyone here. In addition to the broad range of cultural items found at government-run establishments such as **Lak Sala** and **Lak Medura**, take a trip to Colombo's biggest department store, Odels, for just about anything else. Odel's gives Macy's a run for its money, and they even have a great sushi bar.

In addition to several major western-style malls or shopping centers, including **Liberty Plaza** and **Crescat Mall**, there are several independent stores that should not be missed. For textiles, housewares, and hand-loomed clothes visit **Barefoot**, a well-known shop on the bustling Galle Road started by local designer Barbara Sansone. Barefoot may cost more, but its top quality products are still a bargain when converted into dollars or euros. Housed in a renovated colonial-era home complete with a spacious backyard that has been converted into a café/restaurant, you can have a quiet drink or bite to eat while recovering from shopping. **Paradise Road** is another establishment known for truly unique gifts and souvenirs. From incense and candles, to glasses and dishware, this store will also ship some of its heavier items directly to your home so you won't have to lug them back. In a similar vein, the **Gallery Café,** located in the former home of renowned Sri Lankan architect Geoffrey Bawa, has knick-knacks that you will not find anywhere else such as stationery made out of Elephant dung. ❖

# A Cornucopia of
# SPICES
## & Other Essential Ingredients

## Spices & Flavorings

**Asafetida (Perunkayam)** –
A member of the parsley family,
asafetida features more prominently
in South Indian and Tamil cuisine.
The milky juice obtained from the
root forms a brown, resinous mass
when dried, and this pure form is
more potent than the readily available powdered form. Due to its
strong, sometimes offensive odor,
reminiscent of fresh garlic, this is
a spice to be used in moderation.
In fact, just a pinch in the pot is
sufficient. Asafetida is most often
used in the preparation of dhal
(legumes) both as a flavoring and
for its anti-flatulent properties.

**Black mustard seeds (Abba) –**
Round (about 1mm in diameter) and actually dark brown in color, black mustard seeds are derived from a plant that is a member of the cabbage family. Dried, they exhibit no odor, revealing a pungent taste when chewed for a while. Roasted, they take on a grayish appearance, have a pleasant nutty smell, and are far less pungent. Used in a variety of Sri Lankan dishes from pickles and chutneys to dhal and *mallun,* the seeds are also supposed to be a good digestive. Black mustard seeds should not be confused with the brown and white varieties, which are used to make the popular condiment that is an indispensable companion to hot dogs.

**Black Pepper –** See Peppercorns.

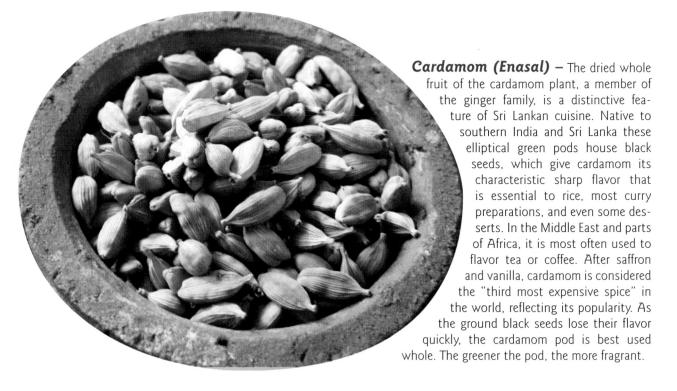

**Cardamom (Enasal) –** The dried whole fruit of the cardamom plant, a member of the ginger family, is a distinctive feature of Sri Lankan cuisine. Native to southern India and Sri Lanka these elliptical green pods house black seeds, which give cardamom its characteristic sharp flavor that is essential to rice, most curry preparations, and even some desserts. In the Middle East and parts of Africa, it is most often used to flavor tea or coffee. After saffron and vanilla, cardamom is considered the "third most expensive spice" in the world, reflecting its popularity. As the ground black seeds lose their flavor quickly, the cardamom pod is best used whole. The greener the pod, the more fragrant.

**Cayenne pepper powder / Chili powder
(Miris kudu)** – Derived from grinding dried red
chilies to a fine powder, Sri Lankan chili powder is
practically synonymous with the cayenne pepper powder
used in the west. It should not, however, be confused
with paprika, which shares its reddish hue but lacks
any bite. Chili/cayenne powder, which provides the
heat in most Sri Lankan curries, should be regulated
accordingly to suite each individual's palate. In moderate
amounts, it promotes good circulation and digestion.

**Cinnamon (Kurundu)** — As the cinnamon tree, a member of the laurel family, is native to Sri Lanka, it is only natural that the island's inhabitants would utilize its outer bark in a variety of dishes—from fragrant biryani to fiery curries, where it is used whole (typically as a 2-inch quill or roll). With a taste both sweet and warming, ground cinnamon is also a constituent of curry powder, whereas in the west it is most often used in desserts.

***Cloves (Karabunati)*** — Dried clove buds go hand in hand with cardamom as a popular spice in Sri Lankan cuisine. These tiny offspring of the clove tree pack a powerful, fragrant punch as well as a sharp, intense flavor and should be used judiciously so as not to overpower other spices. Typically, one or two cloves are used to flavor rice or a curry, and are often removed afterwards. Ground cloves are also used. In Sri Lanka, toothpaste and mouthwash are made with clove oil for its antiseptic properties.

**Coriander (Kottamalli)** – Similar in appearance to its close cousin, parsley, the coriander plant can be used for its leaves, fruit (often called seeds), and roots, each of which possess a very distinct flavor. It is the dried, roasted fruit that comprises one of the main ingredients of curry powder. The fresh leaves, often called "Chinese parsley" or "cilantro," which are popular in Mexican, Thai, and Indian cooking, are rarely used in Sri Lanka. The taste of the coriander fruit/seed can be described as warm, nutty, and almost citrus-like, and a tea made from the powder is used as a remedy for colds or fever.

**Cumin (Suduru)** – Cumin is a popular spice the world over except in the west, where it is often confused with the caraway seed, which it resembles. Another member of the parsley family, the strongly aromatic cumin fruits (called seeds) figure prominently in the multi-spice blend known as curry powder. They are usually toasted or fried in ghee or oil to enhance their sharp flavor and must be used judiciously so as not to overpower the other flavors of a curry. It is also better to stock the whole fruit/seeds and grind just before use to preserve its distinct aroma.

# Ayurveda: The Science of Life

Ayurveda, a Sanskrit term referring to the holistic system of medicine that originated in India between 2500 and 1500 BCE, literally translates to "the science of life." In Hindu mythology, the development of this form of traditional medicine can be attributed to Dhanvantari, physician of the gods. Based on the five elements—earth, water, fire, air, and ether—which make up the universe (the macrocosm) and thus by association the human body (the microcosm), Ayurveda includes a strong metaphysical component as well as practical applications. According to its basic philosophy, a healthy metabolic system with good digestion and proper excretion leads to vitality and longevity. To this end, the emphasis is on preventing disease, rejuvenating the body, and extending the life span.

Nutrition obviously plays a major role with regards to health, and in the Ayurvedic system food is medicine. All food is characterized by six tastes—sweet, sour, salty, bitter, pungent, astringent—that should be present at every meal in order to maintain balance. People, meanwhile, fall under three different elemental energies or doshas: *vata* (air), *pitta* (fire), *kapha* (earth). Each individual possesses a unique combination of these three, but usually favors one. Depending on your dominant dosha, different foods, including herbs and spices, will have either harmful, beneficial, or neutral effects on you. Cinnamon and cardamom, for example, are considered digestive aids, while turmeric is valued for its antiseptic and anti-inflammatory qualities. Ayurveda, in fact, has influenced many traditional dishes in India and Sri Lanka.

As a discipline that addresses mind, body, and spirit, Ayurveda also includes such components as yoga, meditation, and massage. In Sri Lanka today Ayurvedic tourism has grown in popularity as people come for the specific purpose of spending time in Ayurvedic spas or retreats. Even among the locals, Ayurvedic medicine remains as respected as western medicine on the island. I myself have gone to see a traditional healer or '*wedemathaya*,' who was able to permanently vanquish my lower back pain with a poultice of funky-smelling herbs which I wore on the affected area for three days. ❧

***Curry leaves (Karapincha)*** – One of the most essential flavors of Sri Lankan cuisine, the curry leaf is one ingredient that has no substitute (I have seen bay leaves recommended, but the bay leaf bears no similarity in aroma or taste). Not to be confused with the curry plant of southern European origin, the curry tree is indigenous to India, and luckily its fresh leaves may be procured at any Indian store. But be sure to buy them fresh and green as the dried variety will simply not achieve the authentic flavor. They may be stored in the freezer for a few weeks if the leaves stay intact with the stems. Curry leaves are used both fresh and fried in practically every savory Sri Lankan dish, including rice.

***Fennel seeds*** See Sweet cumin

***Fenugreek (Uluhal)*** – A spice from antiquity known for its medicinal properties (as a remedy for flatulence), fenugreek seeds are brownish-yellow and characterized by their bitter flavor (and so used sparingly). The fresh green leaves, prepared like spinach, are also eaten and sometimes utilized in dishes such as crab curry. But Sri Lankan curries favor the seeds, which lose some of their bitterness when toasted. Fenugreek is rich in phosphate, calcium, and iron, and is also said to be good for lowering cholesterol.

**Gamboge (Goraka) –** Gamboge is a popular souring agent/acid in Sri Lankan cuisine. Usually one kidney-shaped segment of the fruit (black when dried) is dissolved in some warm water and then added to the curry. As this fruit is found only in Sri Lanka, the best substitute for it would be tamarind.

*Clockwise from top left: limes, garlic, onions, shallots, ginger, green chilies*

**Garlic (Sudulunu)** – A member of the onion family, garlic is another flavor enhancer known worldwide. Its characteristic strong odor when fresh lessens remarkably upon frying making it the perfect complement to ginger, pepper, chilies, and other spices used in Sri Lankan curries. In addition, garlic contains a whole host of medicinal properties from treating fevers, coughs, and flatulence to disorders of the nervous system and high cholesterol.

**Ginger (Inguru)** – Ginger ranks among the most important and popular spices in the world. A fleshy white rhizome covered by a thick light-brown skin, the pungent flavor and smell of fresh ginger is unmistakable. In Sri Lanka, ginger is mostly used fried, not raw, allowing the warming spicy flavor to give way to a mild, rich taste that blends perfectly with fried garlic and onion. Ginger is also beneficial for digestion.

**Green chili (Amu Miris)** – The unripe stage of the red chili, green chilies provide an added kick to Sri Lankan curries. Though it is almost unthinkable to have Asian food without chili, this plant, along with the tomato and potato, was introduced to Southeast Asia by the Portuguese, who transplanted it from the Americas. Before its arrival, people in this part of the world used only black pepper to add punch to their food.

### Lemongrass (Sera) –
While Thai food is most associated with lemongrass, Sri Lankans also use the white stalks of this indigenous grass to flavor their curries—albeit in more subtle ways. Typically, a small piece of lemongrass will be used as a complement to other ingredients. Thanks to the advent of such specialty supermarkets as Whole Foods, fresh lemongrass is readily available in America.

### Lime (Dehi) –
A lime is to Sri Lankan cooking as a lemon is to Mediterranean cuisine. Used as a souring agent in the preparation of some curries, lime is also liberally squeezed on many dishes before serving.

### Mace (Wasa-vasi) and Nutmeg (Sadikka) –

Nutmeg is the seed of an apricot-like fruit that is native to the Banda Islands, part of the famed "Spice Islands" in Eastern Indonesia. Mace is the arillus, or thin leathery covering that partially shrouds the seed. While the pulp of this fruit is used to make jam in Indonesia, the rest of the world knows nutmeg and mace mainly in their powdered form. Strongly aromatic, both spices are used mostly in desserts in the west, while Sri Lankans use them as a delicate flavoring in certain curries.

### Onion (Lunu) –

Though classified as a vegetable, whose bulbous cluster of leaves grows underground, the onion is probably the oldest and most widely used flavor enhancer. Mentioned in the Old Testament as well as on clay tablets from Mesopotamia, it is an essential ingredient in most every country's cuisine. A raw onion has a spicy and pungent odor and taste, which mellows upon cooking—even to the point of becoming sweet. While slow-cooked in practically every kind of Sri Lankan curry, onions are also added fried along with curry leaves at the end of a preparation in a unique process known as "tempering." Shallots are also employed in Sri Lankan cooking for a finer, less pungent flavor.

**_Pandanus (Rampe)_** – Known as the "screw pine" or "umbrella tree" in English, pandanus leaves are always used fresh (or slightly withered, when their pleasant, nutty odor is evident). While many Asian cultures (Thais, Malays, and Indonesians) use pandanus primarily to flavor rice, Sri Lankans also use a piece in many curry dishes. Because of the scarcity of fresh pandanus in the west and the subtle flavor it imparts, this ingredient could be omitted or else substituted by its essence, which might be found at a Thai store where it is known as _Toey._

***Peppercorns (Gammiris)*** – Peppercorns, the dried fruit (berries) of the pepper plant, are probably one of the most widely used spices in the world. They can be black, white, green, or red depending on the time of harvest and special methods of processing. Native to the Malabar Coast in southern India, pepper became one of the most important spices of antiquity, leading to the opening of more trade routes between east and west. Today, pepper is produced throughout Southeast Asia. It adds a definite kick to food, though not as strong as that of the chili family. In order to assure maximum pungency and aroma, peppercorns are best used freshly ground in a peppermill.

***Red chili (dried) (Vellichemiris)*** – The most popular variety of chili found in Sri Lanka is red in its ripened form, but always sun dried before use, deepening its color and allowing for longer shelf life. This chili is used whole, crushed into flakes, or powdered and is the main source of heat in all the fiery Sri Lankan curries. If spicy is not your style, but you don't want to lose the aesthetic properties of a red curry, use paprika, which has all of the color and none of the kick.

**Saffron** — Saffron holds the honor of being the most expensive spice in the world. The thin red strand is actually the stigma or female sex organ of the crocus sativa flower (a member of the iris family), and it takes approximately 150,000 such flowers to produce one kilo of dried saffron. This fact, along with its very intensive and unique fragrance and slightly bitter taste, make it a spice to use in minute amounts.

**Salt (Diya Lunu)** – Salt is one ingredient universally used by humans to flavor and sometimes preserve their food. In Sri Lanka, home chefs often keep a bowl of brine (salt and water) by the stovetop for this purpose.

***Sweet cumin (Maduru)*** — Otherwise known as fennel seed or anise in the west, the seeds are actually the plants' fruits. While the leaves and stalks of this relative of parsley are eaten as a vegetable in Europe, in Sri Lanka only the dried, toasted fruit/seed is used for curries. Toasting tends to change the flavor of sweet cumin to a more spicy impression making it a suitable addition to curry powder.

**Tamarind (Siyambala)** – Originally from East Africa, tamarind is a fruit known all over the tropics for its intensely tart flavor. The pea-shaped pods can be eaten raw, but for cooking purposes only the pulp is used—usually dissolved in some water and strained of seeds and fiber. Utilized heavily in South Indian and Tamil cooking—along with plenty of chilies—tamarind gives this food its characteristic hot and sour taste and dark color. In Sri Lanka, it is used as a souring agent in a wide variety of meat and fish curries. It can also be used as a substitute for gamboge (goraka).

***Turmeric (Kaha)*** — A member of the ginger family, the turmeric rhizome resembles its cousin in its raw, root-like state. Fresh, it has a spicy, aromatic fragrance, while dried, its odor becomes more medicinal. Along with its many culinary applications, it also has religious significance for Hindus, its yellow hue representing the sun. Turmeric is also used as an antiseptic in Ayurvedic medicine. In Sri Lankan cooking, it is used primarily to add color to dishes such as dhal curry or potatoes.

# Other Essential Ingredients

*Maldive Fish*

**Ghee** – Ghee is clarified butter, which adds a very rich flavor to rice and curry. It is made by simply melting butter and separating the clear residue, suitable for cooking at higher temperatures, where normal butter would burn. While more commonly used in Indian cooking, it is indispensable for a dish like biriyani.

**Maldive fish (Umbalakada)** – Maldive fish is bonito tuna that has been boiled, dried in intense sun until rock-hard, and shredded. As one ingredient specific to Sri Lankan cuisine, it is unlikely that you will find it outside of a store selling Sri Lankan products. It might be worth going out of your way to find it, however, as it adds great flavor and consistency to such dishes as *mallung* and the popular coconut sambol. A suitable substitute would be the small dried shrimp found in Asian grocery stores.

### Coconut milk and Coconut oil (Pol Kiri / Pol Thel)

— One of the essential elements of Sri Lankan cuisine is the coconut, which grows abundantly around the island. The white "meat" and milk, made from macerating the meat and straining it, are used in a variety of dishes. The sap from a certain coconut flower is used to make deliciously sweet pani or treacle (coconut syrup), or fermented and distilled into popular alcoholic beverages like toddy or arrack. The hard brown shells are used to make spoons and bowls, while the rough outer husk is perfect for brushes and brooms. Even the water inside young "king" coconuts is enjoyed as a refreshing drink loaded with electrolytes. But when it comes to cooking, coconut milk and coconut oil account for the lion's share of use. ✿

## *The Merits of the Coconut*

In the health-conscious west, where the consumption of coconut is relatively recent and rather limited to sweets, people harbor many misconceptions about this delicious and very healthy fruit (it is not botanically classified as a nut). To begin with, the coconut acquired a bad rap for its high fat content and the belief that it raises cholesterol levels. But new studies are showing some very promising results. While coconut oil does contain a high percentage of fat, approximately 50 percent of these fatty acids are in the form of lauric acid, a medium chain fatty acid found in human breast milk. These fatty acids are not stored, but sent directly to the liver and converted into energy, actually speeding up the body's metabolism and promoting weight loss. In addition, lauric acid, which is converted into monolaurin in the human body, is anti-viral, anti-bacterial, and anti-fungal, and scientists are finding it effective in treating HIV, herpes, and even common viruses like the flu. Studies have also shown that coconut oil actually reduces overall cholesterol levels if they are high, and increases them if they are low. But don't take my word for it—do a little research for yourself. The information is out there. As Dr. Bruce Fife, author of *The Healing Miracles of Coconut Oil,* says, "Coconut oil is the healthiest oil on Earth." Since Sri Lankan cuisine is practically drenched in coconut milk and coconut oil, go ahead and indulge! ✧

# RECIPES

# Curry Powders

he basic ingredients (and their proportions) of a curry powder vary greatly from one Asian country to another. A curry is also only as good as the mixture of spices used to make it. Store bought varieties just cannot compete with the flavor and aroma of home-made: that's like comparing instant coffee to freshly ground roasted beans. In Sri Lanka, spices are usually bought whole, raw, and in bulk. They are dried out in the sun in handwoven, palm frond baskets before roasting and grinding. Thankfully you don't have to go to such great lengths to get a decent blend. Small packets of seeds purchased at any spice store may be blended in a coffee grinder (dedicated for spices only, of course) and stored in jars in the refrigerator. When made in small batches and properly stored, curry powder can retain its essence for as long as six months.

# Raw Curry Powder

*This basic, unroasted spice mixture is generally used for vegetable curries.*

## Ingredients

- 3 tablespoons coriander seeds
- 3 tablespoons cumin seeds
- 1 ½ tablespoons fennel seeds
- 1 teaspoon turmeric powder

## Preparation

Grind ingredients in coffee grinder and store in a glass jar in the fridge.

**Note:** If you are feeling lazy, no worries. I've done the work for you. You may purchase Skiz's Original Roasted or Raw Curry Powder at the following food sites:

www.foodoro.com
www.foodzie.com

# Roasted Curry Powder

*This roasted spice mixture, used for meat and fish curries, is usually supplemented by healthy doses of Sri Lankan chili powder (cayenne pepper powder) and fresh chilies.*

## Ingredients

- 1 tablespoon uncooked rice
- 4 tablespoons coriander seeds
- 2 tablespoons cumin seeds
- 2 tablespoons fennel seeds
- 2-inch (5-cm) piece cinnamon stick
- ½ teaspoon fenugreek seeds
- 1 teaspoon black peppercorns
- 1 teaspoon black mustard seeds
- 1 teaspoon turmeric powder
- 5 cardamom pods, shelled
- 5 cloves
- 2-inch (5-cm) piece pandanus (optional)
- 2 sprigs curry leaves

## Preparation

Toast each ingredient separately in a saucepan over medium heat, stirring often, until fragrant and browned. Remove from heat, cool, and grind together in a coffee grinder. Store in a glass jar in the fridge.

# Jaffna Curry Powder

*This spicier version of curry powder comes from the north of Sri Lanka, which is predominantly Tamil. The large amount of chilies provides the heat behind many Tamil foods.*

## Ingredients

- *4 ounces dry red chilies*
- *8 tablespoons coriander seeds*
- *2 tablespoons black peppercorns*
- *1 teaspoon turmeric powder*
- *2 sprigs curry leaves*
- *2 tablespoons fennel seeds*
- *1 tablespoon white cumin seeds*
- *1 tablespoon fenugreek seeds*

## Preparation

**1.** Place chilies, coriander seeds, peppercorns, turmeric, and curry leaves in a pan and dry roast until curry leaves are crisp. Roast fennel seeds, white cumin seeds, and fenugreek seeds until golden brown.

**2.** Mix all ingredients together and grind in a coffee grinder. Store in a glass jar in the fridge.

# Curry: What's in a Name?

Today the term "curry" evokes a spice-laden dish with a rich sauce or gravy, but the etymology of the word has a mixed heritage. *"Cury"* comes from the Old English term for cooking, derived from the French *"cuire,"* meaning to cook, boil, or grill. It appears in the title of the first real English cookbook, *"The Forme of Cury,"* commissioned by King Richard II in 1390—obviously long before British contact with Asia. Modern usage of the term "curry" can more likely be traced to the south Indian languages of Kannadan and Malayalam, in which the word *"karil"* is used to alternatively describe a mixture of spices as well as dishes of sautéed meat and vegetables. Similarly, in the Tamil language, *kari* means sauce. Under the Portuguese, who were the first European traders in South Asia, these terms morphed into *"caril"* and *"carree,"* which eventually became "curry" in the British parlance. It should also be noted that the wok-shaped pan in which meals are prepared in India is called a *karahi.*

Despite great regional variations in Indian cooking styles, the British simply adopted "curry" as a generic term for any spicy dish with a thick sauce or gravy. They also invented curry powder as a means for exporting the dishes they fell in love with in India back to the homeland. While Indians are very familiar with masalas, or pre-mixed spice mixtures, usually added at the end of the cooking process, the concept of curry powder was foreign to them. In the typical Indian kitchen, equipped with a grindstone, spices were usually ground and mixed to order, according to whatever dish was being prepared. But as the British came to think of all curries as variations on the same theme, they devised the concept of a standard curry powder, which made it easier for cooks back in England to re-create those beloved Indian dishes. ❖

# Short Eats, Soups & Gravies

*A*s notorious snackers, Sri Lankans enjoy savory 'short eats' any time of day. Such snacks are conveniently sold at bakeries and roadside stalls or kades in Sri Lanka. Unlike traditional appetizers, they are almost never eaten before a main meal because they are so good, you would probably have no room left for dinner! In more urban homes, soups are usually eaten as a light evening meal, and gravies are made to be mopped up with hoppers (moist sourdough pancakes, crispy on the edges) or string hoppers (steamed rice noodles).

# Beef, Fish or Shrimp Patties

*These ground meat or fish-filled pastries make an excellent finger food for cocktail parties or afternoon tea. It remains unclear whether the Portuguese or the British introduced these fine snacks to the island, but they resemble a more refined, delicate, and, of course, spicier version of Britain's Cornish Pasty.*

## Ingredients

**Pastry:**
- 1 pound (454 g) flour
- 1 teaspoon salt
- 3 egg yolks
- 4 tablespoons margarine or shortening
- dash of lemon juice
- 1 egg, beaten

**Filling:**
- See fish, beef, and shrimp filling on page 47

**Makes 10 to 15 patties**

## Cooking Instructions

1. Put flour and salt in a bowl. Make a well in the center and add egg yolks. Mix well, adding margarine and lemon juice. Knead and set aside for about an hour. Heat oven to 350 degrees F (175 degrees C).

2. On a floured surface, roll pastry out thin (about $\frac{1}{8}$-inch to $\frac{1}{4}$-inch thick). Use mouth of a bowl or mug to stamp out rounds about 4 to 5 inches in diameter.

3. Place 1 teaspoon of filling in center of a round and slightly flatten. Wet one semicircle edge with water, and fold pastry over the filling. Use teeth of fork to fuse the two edges together. Brush outside of patty with beaten egg. Repeat with remaining circles of dough.

4. Place the patties on an ungreased baking sheet and bake for 15 minutes at 350 degrees F (175 degrees Celsius). Patties may also be deep-fried.

5. Cool on a wire rack.

*Cutlets made from the fish, beef, and shrimp fillings*

# Filling for Cutlets, Patties, & Chinese Rolls

## Ingredients

### Fish Filling:
- 1 large potato
- 2 tablespoons oil
- 1 onion, finely chopped
- 2 cloves garlic, minced
- 2-inch (5-cm) piece ginger, minced
- 2 to 3 green chilies, finely chopped
- 1 sprig curry leaves
- 1 (6-ounce) can tuna fish (salmon or mackerel may also be used)
- 1 teaspoon cayenne pepper powder
- 1 teaspoon raw curry powder (page 41)
- 1/2 teaspoon ground black pepper
- salt to taste
- juice of 1 lime

### Beef Filling:
- 1 large potato
- 1/2 pound (226 g) ground beef
- 1 onion, finely chopped
- 2 cloves garlic, minced
- 2-inch (5-cm) piece ginger, finely chopped
- 2 to 3 green chilies, finely chopped
- 1 sprig curry leaves
- 1 teaspoon cayenne pepper powder
- 1 teaspoon roasted curry powder (page 41)
- 1/2 teaspoon ground black pepper
- salt to taste

### Shrimp filling:
- 1 large potato
- 2 tablespoons oil
- 1 onion, finely chopped
- 2 cloves garlic, finely chopped
- 2-inch (5-cm) piece ginger, finely chopped
- 2 to 3 green chilies, finely chopped
- 1 sprig curry leaves
- 1 pound (454 g) shrimp, boiled, peeled, and chopped
- 1 teaspoon cayenne pepper powder
- 1 teaspoon roasted curry powder (page 41)
- 1/2 teaspoon ground black pepper
- salt to taste
- juice of 1 lime
- 1 tablespoon coconut milk

## Cooking Instructions

1. Wash, peel, and dice potato. Boil in water until soft. Drain.

2. Heat oil in pan. (Note: if using beef, no oil is necessary as the fat from the beef will be sufficient. Cook beef first and then add other ingredients.) Fry onions until translucent. Add garlic, ginger, green chilies, and curry leaves.

3. Drain any excess liquid and add beef, fish, or shrimp to pan. Add potatoes, cayenne powder, curry powder, pepper, and salt. Toss well and mash potato with spatula. Squeeze in lime juice and add coconut milk if making shrimp filling. Sauté for 3 minutes then set aside to cool.

4. Use for making cutlets (page 51), patties (page 45), or Chinese rolls (page 49).

# Mihiri's Chinese Rolls

*My aunt's neighbor Mihiri is like a one-woman factory when it comes to making these delicious appetizers—dipping them in the batter with one hand and frying them with the other. Despite being somewhat labor-intensive, these crunchy breaded rolls surrounding a moist tasty filling are well worth your efforts. They are called "Chinese" rolls since they closely resemble the traditional egg roll.*

## Ingredients

**Batter:**
- 2 cups (500 ml) flour
- 2 eggs
- 1 cup (250 ml) water
- ½ teaspoon baking powder
- salt to taste

**Filling:**
- See fish, beef, and shrimp fillings on page 47

**Outer coating:**
- 2 cups (500 ml) dry breadcrumbs
- oil for frying

Makes 10 to 15 Chinese rolls

## Cooking Instructions

*1.* Combine all batter ingredients in a blender. Mixture should be on the thick side.

*2.* Brush frying pan with oil. When heated, ladle one spoonful of batter onto pan and swirl around. Pancake should be about ⅛ inch (3 mm) to ¼ inch (6 mm) thick and 5 to 6 inches (12 to 13 cm) in diameter. Repeat until you have made 10 to 15 pancakes, brushing pan with oil after each pancake is removed (reserve leftover batter).

*3.* To assemble rolls, place 1 tablespoon filling on the side of the pancake closest to you, and spread into a line. Fold in the sides first, and then roll. The moisture creates a natural seal. Repeat with remaining pancakes.

*4.* When all the rolls are made, dip each in batter again and coat with breadcrumbs.

*5.* Immerse completely in hot oil and fry until rolls are golden brown. Remove to newspaper to drain excess oil and cool.

**NOTE:** *Chinese rolls may be assembled and stored (frozen) before the breading and frying stage.*

# Beef, Fish or Shrimp Cutlets

*These deep-fried, breaded croquettes made of ground meat or fish and potatoes are sometimes served as an accompaniment to rice and curry. Of course, they can also be the star of the show at a cocktail party or as a savory snack with afternoon tea.*

## Ingredients

**Filling:**
See  fish, beef, and shrimp fillings on page 47

**Coating:**
- 1 beaten egg
- 2 cups (500 ml) dry breadcrumbs
- oil for frying

**Makes 10 to 15 cutlets**

## Cooking Instructions

1. When filling is cool, form into golf ball-size balls.

2. Beat egg in a bowl and dip balls into mixture.

3. Spread out breadcrumbs on a plate or flat surface and coat cutlets completely.

4. Heat oil in a deep pan to 350 degrees F (175 degrees C). (Oil should be deep enough to cover the cutlets.) Deep fry cutlets until golden brown. Drain excess oil and cool slightly on some paper towels. These are best eaten hot.

# Spicy Lentil Fritters *(Masala Vadai)*

*A spicy Asian version of falafel, Vadai, which originated in south India, is made with lentils instead of chickpeas. Crisp on the outside and moist on the inside, this snack provides the perfect cure for the munchies.*

## Ingredients

- 2 cups (500 ml) dry yellow split peas
- 1 onion, chopped
- 4 to 5 green chilies, chopped
- 1-inch (2.5 cm) piece ginger, minced
- 1 teaspoon fennel seeds
- 1 sprig curry leaves, chopped
- salt to taste
- oil for frying

**Makes about 20 *vadai***

## Cooking Instructions

1. Soak split peas in water for at least 6 hours.
2. Wash and grind split peas to a smooth, thick paste.
3. Mix in all other ingredients except the oil.
4. Form mixture into golf-ball-size balls. Cup each ball in both hands and flatten slightly so the middle is thicker than the edges.
5. Deep fry in oil heated to 350 degrees F (175 degrees C) until golden brown. Remove to newspaper or paper towels to drain excess oil and cool slightly. They can be served hot or at room temperature.

# Savory Donuts *(Ulundu Vadai)*

*These savory "donuts" are light and airy on the inside and crispy on the outside. They are made out of lentils (black gram or urad dhal) that may be purchased at any Indian store.*

## Ingredients

- ½ cup (125 ml) lentils (black gram or urad dhal)
- oil for frying
- 1 medium onion, finely chopped
- 2 or 3 green chilies, finely chopped
- 1-inch (2.5 cm) piece ginger, finely chopped
- 1 sprig curry leaves, finely chopped
- 1 teaspoon black mustard seeds
- salt to taste

**Makes about 10 *vadai***

## Cooking Instructions

**1.** Soak the lentils in water for at least 6 hours, changing the water a couple of times.

**2.** Drain lentils and grind to a smooth paste in a food processor.

**3.** Heat about 1 tablespoon oil in pan. Add onions, green chilies, ginger, and curry leaves and fry until onions are golden brown. Add mustard seeds and fry until they start to pop (about a minute).

**4.** Fold tempered ingredients into lentil mixture and add salt to taste. Mix well.

**5.** Heat a large pot of oil for frying. Use approximately a tablespoon of the mixture to form each donut-shaped *vadai*.

**6.** Deep fry, flipping once during cooking, and drain immediately on newspaper. Serve with yogurt or coconut chutney (page 174).

# Spicy Chickpeas *(Kadala))*

*A popular street food, these spicy treats often come served wrapped in a newspaper cone. Since they are so easy to make, healthy, and delicious as well, you can enjoy them at home now too.*

## Ingredients

- 1 (14-ounce) can chickpeas
- 1 tablespoon vegetable oil
- 1 small red onion, finely chopped
- 2 cloves garlic, minced
- 5 whole red chilies, coarsely ground
- 1 sprig curry leaves
- 1 teaspoon mustard seeds
- 1/4 teaspoon turmeric powder
- salt to taste

**Makes 2 to 3 servings**

## Cooking Instructions

**1.** Wash and drain chickpeas.

**2.** Heat oil in pan. Add onions, garlic, chilies, and curry leaves and fry until onions are golden brown. Add mustard seeds and fry until they start to pop, about a minute.

**3.** Add chickpeas, turmeric, and salt, and stir-fry on high for 2 minutes. These may be served hot or at room temperature.

# Jaffna Seafood Soup *(Kool)*

*This very substantial and spicy soup utilizes much of the bountiful seafood of coastal Jaffna, where it originated. Imagine bouillabaisse with a kick! While it might be very difficult to find Palmyra root flour in the west, potato flour should prove a suitable substitute.*

## Ingredients

- ¼ pound (113 g) fish steaks
- ¼ pound (113 g) squid
- ¼ pound (113 g) shrimp
- ¼ pound (113 g) crabs
- ¼ pound (113 g) crayfish
- ¾ cup (185 ml) Palmyra root flour (odiyal) or potato flour
- 1 piece tamarind (lime size)
- ¼ pound (113 g) green beans, cut into 1-inch pieces
- ¼ pound (113 g) yucca or potato, peeled and diced
- ¼ pound (113 g) jackfruit seeds (optional)
- 3 tablespoons uncooked rice
- salt to taste
- 2 tablespoons cayenne pepper powder
- ½ teaspoon turmeric powder
- ¼ pound (113 g) spinach, washed and chopped

## Cooking Instructions

1. Clean and wash all of the seafood. Cut fish and squid into bite-size pieces, shell shrimp, quarter crabs.

2. Soak flour in a cup of water for 10 minutes and drain.

3. Dissolve tamarind in a cup of water and remove seeds.

4. Fill half a large pot with water and bring to a boil.

5. Add fish, squid, shrimp, crabs, crayfish, beans, yucca or potato, jackfruit seeds, rice, and salt and simmer for 45 minutes.

6. In a separate bowl mix soaked flour, tamarind water, cayenne powder, and turmeric powder into a thick paste.

7. Add paste to seafood broth, mix well and simmer until it thickens.

8. Stir in chopped spinach just before removing pot from heat.

**Makes 6 servings**

# Spicy Coriander Tamarind Broth *(Rasam)*

*Another Jaffna Tamil specialty, this broth is actually sipped before or during meals as it is considered an excellent digestive.*

## Ingredients

- *3 tablespoons coriander seeds*
- *1 teaspoon white cumin seeds*
- *1 teaspoon black peppercorns*
- *1 clove garlic, crushed*
- *1 dry red chili, crushed*
- *4 cups (1 liter) water*
- *1 small piece tamarind pulp (marble-size)*
- *salt to taste*

## Cooking Instructions

**1.** Crush the coriander seeds, cumin seeds, and peppercorns and combine with garlic and chili. Place mixture in a pan with water and tamarind and bring to a boil.

**2.** Remove from heat and serve hot.

Makes 4 servings

# Buying, Cracking & Milking a Coconut

*While the coconut is still not a standard item in most grocery stores in the west, you should definitely be able to find one at any Asian or Caribbean store. Luckily, most coconuts available in the U.S. have been stripped of their outer husk to reveal a shaggy brown sphere approximately the size of a small bowling ball.*

  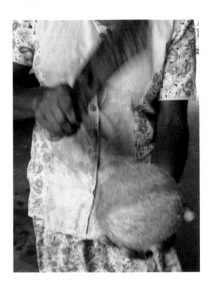

## Buying:

1. Select a coconut with no visible cracks or punctures. There should be no moisture leaking from the "eyes" (three depressions located at the center of the coconut) and these "eyes" should not appear dark or moldy.

2. Hold the coconut in your hands and shake it. It should feel heavy, and there should be some liquid sloshing around inside. No liquid indicates that the coconut is overripe and will not taste good.

## Cracking:

1. Hold the coconut over a large bowl to catch the water that will come out.

2. Find the seam that runs between the 'eyes' of the coconut.

3. Using the blunt end of a heavy cleaver or knife, firmly tap on this seam as you slowly rotate the coconut in the palm of your hand. If done correctly, the coconut will split open in two exact halves. If it cracks but does not open fully, drain all the water into the bowl first, and then place the coconut on a cutting board. Wedge the sharp end of the knife into

the crack and pound the whole coconut on the cutting board to crack the coconut in half. The coconut 'meat' should be nice and white. If it has started to yellow that means the coconut is probably rancid.

A whole coconut may be stored in the fridge for up to 2 months. Once cut, however, the white coconut "meat" will only keep for a few days in the fridge. If you grate the meat and freeze it, it will last for 8 to 10 months.

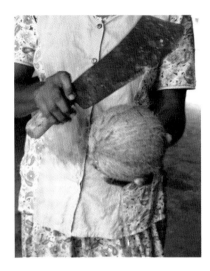

Nothing beats the flavor and aroma of freshly squeezed coconut milk. But if you don't want to go through all the trouble, canned coconut milk is readily available these days at most grocery stores.

## Making Coconut Milk:

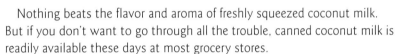

1. Preheat your oven to 400 degrees F for 15 minutes. Put both halves of the cracked coconut in the oven and bake for no more than 10 minutes.

2. Remove coconut halves and allow to cool before separating the white 'meat' from the shell with a knife. You may also peel off the brown skin on the shell side.

3. Break the coconut meat into smaller pieces and shred in a food processor.

4. Transfer the shredded coconut to a large bowl and add 2 cups of boiling water. Steep for 10 minutes and then strain the liquid through a fine mesh strainer into another bowl. Gather the remaining pulp in your hands and squeeze out all the remaining liquid, which will be the creamiest part of the extraction.

5. Add another 2 cups of boiling water to the pulp and repeat the process.

# Coconut Milk Gravy *(Kiri Hodhi)*

*This "gravy" is actually the basis for many vegetable curries. It can also be poured over string hoppers or pittu as a light but tasty sauce. It is quite popular with children because of its mild flavor.*

## Ingredients

- *1 onion, chopped*
- *2 green chilies, sliced*
- *1 sprig curry leaves*
- *2-inch (5 cm) stalk lemongrass*
- *2-inch (5 cm) cinnamon stick*
- *2-inch (5 cm) piece pandanus grass (optional)*
- *½ teaspoon fenugreek seeds*
- *¼ teaspoon turmeric powder*
- *½ cup (125 ml) water*
- *1½ cups (375 ml) coconut milk*
- *½ teaspoon lemon or lime juice*
- *salt to taste*

**Makes 4 servings**

## Cooking Instructions

**1.** Combine all ingredients (except coconut milk, juice, and salt) in a pan. Bring to a boil.

**2.** Add coconut milk and stir well. Simmer for 5 minutes.

**3.** Cool slightly and then add lemon or lime juice and salt.

*Young "king" coconuts are popular for their refreshing water*

# Mulligatawny

*This hearty South Indian soup gets the Sri Lankan treatment with the addition of coconut milk, raw curry powder, and tempered ingredients prior to serving.*

## Ingredients

- 2 tablespoons oil
- 1 large onion, chopped
- 2 pounds (1kg) chicken or mutton with bones, chopped
- 4 cloves garlic, sliced
- 2-inch (5-cm) piece ginger, sliced
- 10 black peppercorns
- 3 tablespoons raw curry powder (page 41)
- ½ teaspoon turmeric powder
- 8 to 10 cups (2 liters) water
- 1 carrot, chopped
- ½ pound (250 g) tomatoes, diced
- 1 cup (250 ml) coconut milk
- salt to taste
- dash of lime juice

*For tempering:*
- 2 tablespoons oil
- 1 onion, chopped
- 1 sprig curry leaves
- 2 teaspoons raw curry powder (page 41)

**Makes 3 to 4 servings**

## Cooking Instructions

1. Heat oil in pan. When hot, fry onions until translucent.

2. Add chicken, garlic, ginger, peppercorns, curry powder, and turmeric powder, and toss for 2 to 3 minutes.

3. Add water, carrot, and tomatoes and bring to boil. Reduce heat and simmer for about 1 hour until stock is reduced to half.

4. Remove meat, cut into small pieces, and discard bones. Return meat to pot and add coconut milk and salt to taste.

5. Just before serving, fry the tempering ingredients in a small skillet and add to pot, stirring well. Add a dash of lime juice before serving.

# Lentil Soup

*Lentils or dhal, as they are known in Sri Lanka and India, are a favorite accompaniment to rice, the staple of the Sri Lankan diet. But this tasty soup, packed with protein, stands on its own when served with bread and a salad.*

## Ingredients

- 8 ounces (226 g) red lentils
- 2 tablespoons oil
- 1 onion, chopped
- 2 cloves garlic, minced
- 2-inch (5-cm) piece ginger, chopped
- 1 sprig curry leaves
- 1 tomato, peeled and chopped
- 2 tablespoons raw curry powder (page 41)
- 1 teaspoon turmeric powder
- ½ teaspoon cayenne pepper powder
- 4 cups (1 liter) water
- 1 cup (250 ml) coconut milk
- salt to taste

**Makes 4 servings**

## Cooking Instructions

**1.** Wash and soak lentils for 30 minutes. Drain water.

**2.** Heat oil in pan. Sauté onions, garlic, ginger, curry leaves, and tomato until onions are translucent.

**3.** Add curry powder, turmeric powder, cayenne powder, lentils and water and bring to a boil. Reduce heat and simmer until lentils are fully cooked (soft).

**4.** Add coconut milk and salt. Cook for an additional 5 minutes.

# Rice & Bread

*A*s the staple food of Sri Lanka and most of Asia, rice is the main component of any meal, and curries are considered mere condiments to eat with it. Sri Lankans grow over twenty different kinds of rice, but the most popular are basmati, a fragrant, long-grain variety, and samba, a short-grain rice more commonly found on the table. Breads are not as common in Sri Lanka as they are in India, but are usually served as an alternative to rice for the evening meal.

# Basic Rice

*This simple preparation, taught to me by my mother, will never fail to produce perfect, fluffy rice every time—especially nice if you don't own a rice cooker.*

## Ingredients

- *1 cup (250 ml) basmati rice*
- *2 tablespoons oil (for more flavor, use butter or ghee)*
- *1 onion, chopped*
- *1 sprig curry leaves*
- *1 cardamom pod*
- *1 clove*
- *2-inch (5-cm) piece pandanus (optional)*
- *2 cups (500 ml) water*
- *1 teaspoon salt or 1 bouillon cube*
- *2 ounces (55 g) cashews*
- *2 ounces (55 g) raisins*

### Makes 2 to 4 servings

## Cooking Instructions

**1.** Wash and drain rice. Set aside.

**2.** Heat oil in medium pot. Fry onions until translucent. Add curry leaves, cardamom pod, clove, and pandanus.

**3.** Stir in rice, and fry for an additional 2 minutes.

**4.** Add the water (it should reach a level approximately one-inch higher than the rice; if you stick your finger in the pot until it touches the surface of the rice, the water should reach to your first finger joint.)

**5.** Bring to a boil. Dissolve salt or bouillon in pot and stir. Reduce heat, cover pot and simmer for about 20 minutes.

**6.** Once water has been absorbed, remove cover and simmer an additional 5 minutes, making sure that rice does not burn and stick to the bottom of the pot.

**7.** In another pan, sauté cashews and raisins in some oil and sprinkle over rice as a garnish.

**Note:** If using brown rice, add an additional ¼ cup (65 ml) water, as this slightly harder rice requires more moisture for cooking.

# Yellow Rice *(Kaha Bath)*

*This fragrant rice gets its color from turmeric and its deep flavor from the chicken stock, ghee, and spices. It is usually served on more festive occasions in Sri Lanka, but go ahead, celebrate life!*

## Ingredients

- 2 cups (500 ml) basmati rice
- 2 tablespoons butter or ghee
- 1 onion, chopped
- 1 sprig curry leaves
- 4 cardamom pods
- 4 cloves
- 1 teaspoon turmeric powder
- 2-inch (5-cm) stalk lemongrass
- 2-inch (5-cm) cinnamon stick
- 2 teaspoons salt
- 2½ cups (625 ml) chicken stock
- 1 cup (250 ml) water

**Makes 4 to 6 servings**

## Cooking Instructions

**1.** Wash and drain rice. Set aside.

**2.** Heat butter or ghee in a medium pot. Fry onion until translucent. Add rice, curry leaves, and all other ingredients except the stock and water. Stir-fry for 2 minutes.

**3.** (You can put mixture into a rice cooker at this point if desired.) Pour in stock and water and bring to a boil. Reduce heat, cover and simmer until liquid evaporates.

**4.** Stir well as spices will emerge on top. They may be removed or kept as a garnish.

# Milk Rice *(Kiri Bath)*

*This unique rice preparation is usually served for breakfast or on auspicious occasions such as weddings or Sri Lankan New Year. It is accompanied by* Lunu miris *(Onion Chili Sambol, page 164),* Seeni sambol *(Sugar Sambol, page 161), and curries, or it may get the sweet treatment with some jaggery (palm sugar) on the side.*

## Ingredients

- 2 cups (500 ml) long-grain rice
- 1½ cups (375 ml) water
- 2 cups (500 ml) coconut milk
- 2 teaspoons salt

**Makes 4 to 6 servings**

## Cooking Instructions

**1.** Wash rice and place in pot or rice cooker.

**2.** Add water, bring to a boil, reduce heat and simmer for 10 minutes.

**3.** Add coconut milk and salt and stir well.

**4.** Cook on low heat for 15 minutes or until liquid has been absorbed.

**5.** Spoon rice onto a plate and flatten to a disc-shape about 2 inches thick. Cut into diamond-shaped slices and serve.

# Ghee Rice *(Ghee Thel Bath)*

*Ghee, or clarified butter, lends itself well to the richness of this rice dish. Lamb stock and ingredients such as lemon also add loads of flavor.*

## Ingredients

- *2 cups (500 ml) basmati rice*
- *3 tablespoons ghee*
- *1 onion, chopped*
- *1 sprig curry leaves*
- *1 teaspoon coriander powder*
- *2-inch (5-cm) stalk lemongrass*
- *2-inch (5-cm) cinnamon stick*
- *4 cardamom pods*
- *4 cloves*
- *4 black peppercorns*
- *2½ cups (625 ml) lamb stock*
- *½ cup (125 ml) water*
- *½ cup (125 ml) yogurt*
- *2 teaspoons salt*
- *2 ounces (55 g) cashew nuts*
- *2 ounces (55 g) raisins*

**Makes 4 to 6 servings**

## Cooking Instructions

**1.** Wash and drain rice. Set aside.

**2.** Heat ghee in medium pot. Fry onions, curry leaves, coriander powder, lemongrass, cinnamon stick, cardamom pods, cloves, and peppercorns until onions are translucent. Add rice and toss for another 2 to 3 minutes. Remove to rice cooker at this point if using.

**3.** Add stock, water, yogurt, and salt and cook until liquid evaporates. Stir well as spices emerge on top.

**4.** Fry the cashew nuts and raisins in a small amount of oil and use to garnish the rice.

# Vegetable Fried Rice *(Elolu Bath)*

*Whenever my mother couldn't get us to eat our vegetables, she would chop them up small and serve them in this Sri Lankan version of fried rice.*

## Ingredients

- 4 tablespoons ghee or butter
- 1 spring onion, finely chopped
- 1 leek, finely chopped
- 1 carrot, grated
- 1 celery stalk, finely chopped
- 1 onion, finely chopped
- 2 cloves garlic, minced
- 2-inch (5-cm) piece ginger, minced
- 1 green chili, minced
- 1 sprig curry leaves
- 2 eggs, beaten
- 6 cups (1.5 liters) cooked rice
- 4 cardamom pods
- 4 cloves
- salt to taste

**Makes 6 to 8 servings**

## Cooking Instructions

**1.** Heat ghee or butter in a pan. Fry vegetables, garlic, ginger, chili, and curry leaves until onions are translucent.

**2.** Add eggs and scramble in pan. Add rice, cardamom pods, cloves, and salt and mix well and heat through.

# Chicken Biryani

*A staple at weddings, this Muslim favorite is usually served with a hard-boiled egg, mint sambol (page 165), and raita (a yogurt and cucumber dressing).*

## Ingredients

*Chicken:*
- 2 pounds (1 kg) chicken parts
- 2 teaspoons salt
- 1 teaspoon ground black pepper
- 1 teaspoon curry powder (page 41)
- 1 teaspoon cayenne pepper powder or paprika
- ¼ cup (65 ml) plain yogurt
- ¼ cup (65 ml) tomato puree
- 2 tablespoons chopped cashews
- 2 tablespoons desiccated coconut
- 1 cardamom pod
- 1 clove
- 2 bay leaves
- 2 tablespoons ghee
- 1 onion, chopped
- 2 Serrano chilies, chopped

*Rice:*
- 1 pound (454 g) basmati rice
- 3 tablespoons ghee
- 1 onion, chopped
- 2 cardamom pods
- 2 cloves
- 2 bay leaves
- 1-inch (2.5-cm) cinnamon stick
- pinch of saffron
- 1½ to 2 cups (375 to 500 ml) chicken stock
- 1½ teaspoons salt

**Makes 6 servings**

## Cooking Instructions

*Chicken:*
1. Wash and dry chicken. Season with salt, black pepper, curry powder, and cayenne powder.
2. In a food processor, blend yogurt, tomato puree, cashews, and coconut.
3. Combine blended ingredients, cardamom pods, clove, and bay leaves with chicken and marinate for 30 minutes. Meanwhile prepare rice (below).
4. Heat oven to 300 degrees F (150 degrees C). Heat ghee in a pan. Fry onions and chilies until onions are translucent.
5. Remove chicken from marinade (reserving marinade), add to pan and stir-fry for 5 to 10 minutes.
6. Add a little water to marinade and pour over chicken. Simmer for 15 to 20 minutes.
7. Place chicken pieces in casserole dish.

*Rice:*
1. Wash and drain rice.
2. Heat ghee in pan. Fry onions until translucent. Add cardamom pods, cloves, bay leaves, and cinnamon stick.
3. Add rice and fry for a few minutes until rice starts to crackle. Add pinch of saffron and mix well.
4. Pour in stock and simmer until rice is partially cooked (about 15 minutes). Add salt.
5. Place rice on top of chicken in casserole dish. Cover with aluminum foil and bake in heated oven until moisture evaporates, about 25 to 30 minutes.

# Lamb Biryani

*A legacy of the Moghuls, whose empire was centered around what is now Pakistan, this rich, delicious dish is usually reserved for special occasions or a Sunday lunch. It's amazing how such a little saffron goes such a long way in flavoring this dish.*

## Ingredients

- *1½ pounds (675 g) basmati rice*
- *1 pound (454 g) lamb or goat (mutton)*
- *⅓ cup (75 ml) plain yogurt*
- *3 teaspoons cumin powder*
- *3 tablespoons ghee*
- *2 onions, chopped*
- *4 cloves garlic, sliced*
- *1-inch (2.5-cm) piece ginger, chopped*
- *6 cardamom pods*
- *6 cloves*
- *2-inch (5-cm) cinnamon stick*
- *2 bay leaves*
- *salt to taste*
- *pinch of saffron*

**Makes 6 servings**

## Cooking Instructions

1. Wash and soak rice for 15 minutes. Drain and set aside.

2. Cut meat into cubes and marinate in yogurt mixed with cumin powder for 20 to 30 minutes.

3. Heat ghee in a medium pot. When hot, fry onions, garlic, ginger, cardamom pods, cloves, cinnamon stick, and bay leaves until onions are translucent.

4. Add meat and some salt and stir-fry to brown.

5. Add rice and stir-fry for 2 to 3 minutes until it begins to crackle.

6. Pour in enough water to cover contents of pan plus 1 inch. Cover and simmer for about 20 minutes until rice is tender and all water is absorbed.

7. Add a pinch of saffron and stir well. Cook on low heat an additional 5 to 10 minutes or until moisture evaporates.

# Shrimp Biryani

*Shrimp biryani is not a very common dish in Sri Lanka, but it offers a seafood version of biryani for those who don't eat meat.*

## Ingredients

**Shrimp:**
- 1 pound (454 g) shrimp with shells
- ¼ cup (65 ml) plain yogurt
- 4 cloves garlic, chopped
- 2-inch (5-cm) piece ginger, chopped
- 10 to 12 cashew nuts, ground
- 8 cardamom pods
- 2 teaspoons cayenne pepper powder
- ¼ teaspoon turmeric powder
- 1½ teaspoons roasted curry powder (page 41)
- 1 teaspoon salt
- 2 tablespoons ghee
- 1 onion, chopped
- 1 sprig curry leaves
- 2-inch (5-cm) cinnamon stick
- 2-inch (5-cm) piece pandanus (optional)
- 3 small tomatoes, diced

**Rice:**
- 1 pound (454 g) basmati rice
- 2 tablespoons ghee
- 1 onion, sliced
- 1 sprig curry leaves
- 4 cardamom pods
- 4 cloves
- 2-inch (5-cm) piece pandanus (optional)
- 2-inch (5-cm) cinnamon stick
- salt to taste

## Cooking Instructions

**1.** Wash and drain shrimp.

**2.** Combine yogurt with garlic, ginger, cashews, cardamom pods, cayenne powder, turmeric powder, curry powder, and salt. Add the shrimp and marinate for 20 to 30 minutes.

**3.** Heat ghee in a pan and fry onions until translucent. Add curry leaves, cinnamon stick, and pandanus. Add shrimp mixture and tomatoes and stir-fry for 3 to 4 minutes. Set aside. Heat oven to 300 degrees F (150 degrees C).

**4.** Make rice: Wash and drain rice. Heat ghee in medium pot and fry onions, curry leaves, and spices until onions are golden brown. Add rice and stir-fry for 2 minutes. Add water to cover the rice plus 1 inch. Cover and simmer for 15 minutes, until half cooked (there will still be some water left).

**5.** Place rice with any water left in a casserole dish (9x13x3) and combine with shrimp. Cover with aluminum foil and cook in oven for about 25 to 30 minutes.

**Makes 6 servings**

# South Indian Specialties:
## Hoppers, String Hoppers & Pittu

**D**ue to the island's close proximity to India, it comes as no surprise that Sri Lankan cuisine bears the unmistakable influence of its neighbor. In fact, some of the most popular foods in Sri Lanka today—hoppers, string hoppers, and *pittu*—trace their origins to the South Indian states of Kerala and Tamil Nadu, which also boast some of the spiciest food on the planet. To accompany all those fiery curries, someone had to come up with something besides rice, which is usually reserved for lunch, the main meal in Sri Lanka, and these three south Indian specialties fit the bill deliciously.

*Hoppers*

Hoppers (an English corruption of the Sinhala *appa*) could be considered a street food in Sri Lanka as they are available any time of day at ubiquitous glass-framed stalls. Made from fermented rice flour, which is cooked in a tiny wok-shaped pan called an *appa-chatti,* these sourdough crepe-like breads are crispy on the edges and moist in the middle. They are usually eaten for breakfast or dinner with a meat or fish curry, some *lunu miris* (a chili and onion condiment, page 164), or just coconut *sambol* (page 163). Though fairly easy to prepare, rarely does anyone in Sri Lanka make them at home anymore since they are so readily available and cheap.

*String Hoppers*

Delicate, steamed rice noodles or string hoppers (*idiyappam* in Sinhala), on the other hand, are usually bought because they are very labor intensive to make. First, rice flour must be steamed; then combined with salt and water to make a dough, which is typically fed through a hand press. Fine noodles are then squeezed out in a circular pattern on coaster-sized bamboo mats and steamed. The resulting moist and light "strings" are customarily doused with a mild coconut milk gravy before eating. They are also served with various curries. String hoppers are one of the first foods I seek out

*Pittu*

after landing in Colombo, and I usually don't have to go very far to find them.

Another popular rice substitute, made with rice flour and shredded coconut, is *pittu,* which is similarly labor intensive. This time the rice flour must be roasted first and combined with shredded coconut. This granular mixture is stuffed into bamboo tubes and steamed, forming its signature cylindrical shape. While it's tricky getting the consistency right, a good *pittu* crumbles easily and soaks up a curry gravy like a sponge.

Of course, all kinds of Indian foods are popular in Sri Lanka—from rich *biriyanis* to savory *idlis,* the disk-shaped cakes made from fermented black lentils, to Bombay sweets—but hoppers, string hoppers, and *pittu* have so firmly entrenched themselves into the lexicon of Sri Lankan cuisine that we consider them our own. ✤

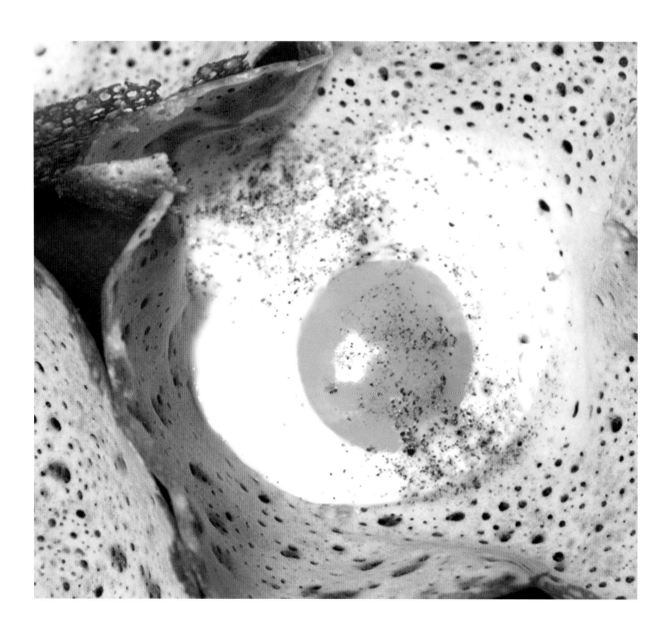

# Hoppers *(Appa)*

*These sourdough pancakes, originally from South India, are popular for both breakfast and dinner in Sri Lanka, and can be bought at ubiquitous roadside stands. They are made in an appachatti, a small curved pan resembling a tiny wok. As the batter is swirled around the sides and cooks it acquires a crispy edge while remaining moist in the middle. Accompaniments include curries with gravy and Lunu miris (Onion Chili Sambol, page 164).*

## Ingredients

- *1 teaspoon dry yeast*
- *¼ cup (65ml) lukewarm water*
- *1 pound (454 g) all-purpose or rice flour*
- *salt to taste*
- *⅛ teaspoon sugar*
- *2½ cups (625 ml) coconut milk (slightly more if using rice flour)*
- *¼ teaspoon baking soda*
- *3 tablespoons oil*

**Makes 10 to 12 hoppers**

## Cooking Instructions

**1.** Dissolve yeast in the lukewarm water. Sift flour into a bowl. Add salt, sugar, yeast mixture and mix well to form a stiff dough. Set aside to rise for 2 to 3 hours.

**2.** Add the coconut milk and a pinch of baking soda to the dough and set aside for another hour. Mix well.

**3.** Oil a hopper pan (or similar spherical pan) and heat over medium flame. Pour in a spoonful of batter and rotate pan so whole surface is covered. Cook until hopper is crispy around the edges (about 2 minutes). Continuing making hoppers, oiling pan after each hopper is made.

**Variation:** For an egg hopper, after pouring batter into pan, break an egg in the center and cover and cook until done.

# Coconut Flat Bread *(Pol Roti)*

*This delicious alternative to rice is eaten for breakfast or dinner. It is usually accompanied by* lunu miris *(Onion Chili Sambol, page 164), chicken, fish or beef curry, or simply butter and a banana. Rotis may be made in larger quantities and frozen for later use. Then just pop them in the toaster for an instant breakfast or dinner.*

## Ingredients

- *8 ounces (226 g) white wheat flour or roasted rice flour*
- *12 ounces (340 g) grated coconut*
- *salt to taste*
- *water*

### Optional:
- *1 onion, chopped*
- *2 to 3 green chilies, chopped*
- *1 tablespoon Maldive fish*

**Makes 4 *rotis***

## Cooking Instructions

**1.** Mix flour, coconut, and salt together in a bowl with a little water to make a stiff dough, adding any optional ingredients.

**2.** Knead well and set aside for 30 minutes.

**3.** Make lime-size balls and flatten to about 5 to 6 inches (13 to 15 cm) in diameter.

**4.** Coat pan with a little oil and cook the *roti* on each side for 2 to 3 minutes until slightly browned.

*Gothamba roti is sometimes stuffed with a meat or fish filling (right)*

# Gothamba Flat Breads *(Gothamba Roti)*

Gothamba roti *is one of the more popular breads in Sri Lanka, and you will find men at streetside stalls expertly preparing the dough and flipping it around like a pizza. In addition to stuffing the* roti *with various meat or fish fillings, it is also chopped up into thin strips and mixed with vegetables, meat, eggs, and spices for the popular street food known as "kotthu."*

## Ingredients

- *2 cups (500 ml) all-purpose flour*
- *1 teaspoon salt*
- *1 cup (250 ml) water*
- *2 to 3 cups (500 to 750 ml) vegetable oil*

**Makes 8 *rotis***

## Cooking Instructions

*1.* In a large bowl combine flour and salt and mix well. Stir in the water to form a dough, and knead for a minute. Add more flour if the dough's consistency is too sticky.

*2.* Roll into a ball. Divide the ball into 8 equal-size dough balls. Place balls in a deep dish and coat with a little oil. Set aside for 2 hours.

*3.* On a clean, flat surface pound dough balls into thin flat rounds.

*4.* Heat oil in pan and cook the dough disks for approximately 1 minute per side.

**Variation:** To make egg gothamba, as one side of the *roti* cooks, crack an egg in the center. Then fold over the edges and flip until the other side is fully cooked.

# Indian Breads

*T*hese South Indian flat breads have become popular in Sri Lanka as an alternative to rice, and are conveniently available at numerous street stalls. However, if you don't happen to have one near you, the good news is that they are very easy to make.

# Chapati

*An Indian flat bread that is popular in Sri Lanka,* chapatis *have become a ubiquitous street food because they are cheap and easy to make.*

## Ingredients

- *8 ounces (226 g) all-purpose flour*
- *salt to taste*
- *oil*

## Cooking Instructions

1. Sift the flour into a bowl and add salt. Mix in a little cold water and work until mixture forms a firm dough. Knead the dough and form into one big ball. Cover with damp cloth and set aside for 1 hour.

2. Make lime-size balls out of the dough. Flatten by hand into discs about ⅛ (3mm) to ¼ inch (6mm) thick and 5 inch (13 cm) in diameter.

3. Cook both sides on a hot, oiled griddle.

Makes 4 *chapatis*

# Dosai

*These savory pancakes of South Indian origin have become a national dish in Sri Lanka. They may be eaten with various curries. Undu flour, made from a type of lentil called black gram, may be purchased at any Indian store or on the Internet.*

## Ingredients

- *1 teaspoon sugar*
- *1½ teaspoons dry yeast*
- *8 ounces (226 g) undu flour*
- *8 ounces (226 g) white wheat flour*
- *1 cup (250 ml) coconut milk*
- *oil*

### For tempering:
- *1 onion, chopped*
- *3 or 4 dry red chilies, chopped*
- *1 sprig curry leaves*
- *½ teaspoon fenugreek seeds*
- *½ teaspoon mustard seeds*
- *2 tablespoons oil*

> **Makes 8 *dosai***

## Cooking Instructions

**1.** Soak sugar and yeast in a little lukewarm water for 5 minutes.

**2.** Mix undu and wheat flour with yeast mixture. Cover and set aside. When mixture doubles in size, add coconut milk. The resulting batter should be of pouring consistency.

**3.** Fry the tempering ingredients in the oil and add to batter.

**4.** Heat an 8-inch skillet and brush with a little oil. Use about ⅓ cup (80 ml) of batter per *dosai* and spread uniformly across pan. When small holes start appearing on the surface flip pancake and cook other side for 1 to 2 minutes.

# Meat & Poultry

# Chicken Curry (Kukul Mas)

*A mainstay of Sri Lankan cuisine, this dish was the first curry I learned to make. Like any curry, its flavor is greatly enhanced the longer it has been marinating prior to cooking, and it tastes even better the next day. I use thighs with the bone in when I make this dish as breast meat tends to dry out.*

## Ingredients

- *1 whole fryer chicken, cut into parts*
- *3 tablespoons roasted curry powder (page 41)*
- *1 to 2 teaspoons cayenne pepper powder*
- *1 teaspoon apple cider vinegar*
- *2 tablespoons oil*
- *1 large onion, chopped*
- *4 cloves garlic, sliced*
- *2-inch (5-cm) piece ginger, chopped*
- *1 sprig curry leaves*
- *2-inch (5-cm) stalk lemongrass*
- *3 cardamom pods*
- *3 cloves*
- *1-inch (2.5-cm) cinnamon stick*
- *1 cup (250 ml) coconut milk*
- *salt to taste*
- *1 tablespoon tomato paste*

**Makes 6 servings**

## Cooking Instructions

**1.** Wash and clean chicken, removing most fat and split the thighs, breasts, and legs.

**2.** Place chicken in bowl with curry powder, cayenne powder, and vinegar. Mix well with hands and set aside for at least 30 minutes. NOTE: Marinate the chicken overnight for optimum results.

**3.** In a large pot, heat oil. Once hot, add onions, garlic, ginger, curry leaves, lemongrass, cardamom pods, cloves, and cinnamon stick. Fry until onions are golden brown.

**4.** Add chicken pieces one by one, stirring occasionally until chicken is browned.

**5.** Add a little water to the bowl that contained the chicken and slosh around to catch any remaining marinade and add to pot. Cover and cook on medium heat for 20 minutes.

**6.** Stir in coconut milk and some salt and bring to a boil. Reduce heat, cover and simmer for an additional 15 minutes.

**7.** Stir in tomato paste and simmer for an additional 2 minutes.

# Pork Curry *(Ooroomas Curry)*

*The key to a good pork curry, according to my Aunt Dora, is to cut the meat into thick chunks and leave all the fat on. "That's where the flavor is," she says. Of course, the tamarind also adds a nice tangy note to the overall spiciness.*

## Ingredients

- 1 tablespoon tamarind pulp*
- 3 tablespoons roasted curry powder (page 41)
- 2 pounds (1 kg) boneless pork
- 2 teaspoons cayenne pepper powder
- 2 tablespoons oil
- 1 large onion, chopped
- 4 cloves garlic, chopped
- 2-inch (5-cm) piece ginger, ground
- 2-inch (5-cm) cinnamon stick
- 2-inch (5-cm) stalk lemongrass
- 2 green chilies, sliced
- 1 sprig curry leaves
- 1½ cups (375 ml) water
- 2 teaspoons salt
- ½ cup (125 ml) coconut milk
- 1 tablespoon tomato paste

Makes 6 servings

## Cooking Instructions

**1.** Soak tamarind in a little warm water; strain and remove seeds and fiber. Slightly toast curry powder in a pan for 2 to 3 minutes.

**2.** Wash and cut pork into 1-inch (2.5-cm) cubes. Place in a bowl with curry powder, cayenne powder, and tamarind and marinate for 30 minutes.

**3.** Heat oil in a pan. When hot, fry onions, garlic, ginger, cinnamon stick, lemongrass, green chilies, and curry leaves for a few minutes.

**4.** Add marinated pork and stir-fry until browned. Slosh a little water in marinade bowl to release the remaining spice mixture and pour into pan. Add remaining water and salt and bring to a boil.

**5.** Reduce heat, cover and simmer until pork is tender (about 20-25 minutes).

**6.** Add coconut milk and tomato paste and simmer, uncovered, until gravy is thick, about 15 to 20 minutes.

**\*Note:** You may use tamarind concentrate instead of pulp, in which case use only about ½ teaspoon as it is strong.

# Beef Curry *(Harak Mas Curry)*

*As the majority of Sri Lankans are either Buddhist or Hindu, beef is not a very popular option on the island. Cutting the beef into smaller cubes allows the meat to tenderize easier as it slow cooks in its rich gravy.*

## Ingredients

- 3 tablespoons roasted curry powder (page 41)
- ½ teaspoon fenugreek seeds
- 2 pounds (1 kg) beef, cut into 1-inch (2.5-cm) cubes
- 1 to 2 teaspoons cayenne pepper powder
- 1 teaspoon paprika
- 2 teaspoons apple cider vinegar
- 2 tablespoons oil
- 1 large onion, chopped
- 4 cloves garlic, sliced
- 2-inch (5-cm) piece ginger, ground
- 2 green chilies, sliced
- 1 sprig curry leaves
- 2-inch (5-cm) stalk lemongrass
- 2-inch (5-cm) cinnamon stick
- 2 cardamom pods
- 2 cloves
- 1 cup (250 ml) water
- 1 cup (250 ml) coconut milk
- salt to taste
- 1 tablespoon tomato paste

Makes 6 to 8 servings

## Cooking Instructions

1. Slightly toast curry powder and fenugreek seeds in a small pan. Mix with beef, cayenne powder, paprika, and vinegar and marinate for at least 1 to 2 hours (or overnight, for optimum results).

2. Heat oil in pan. Sauté onions, garlic, ginger, green chilies, curry leaves, lemongrass, cinnamon stick, cardamom pods, and cloves until onions are translucent.

3. Add marinated beef and stir-fry for several minutes until beef is browned.

4. Slosh a little water in marinating bowl to release the remaining spice mixture and add to pan. Add remaining water and bring to a boil. Reduce heat, cover and simmer for 30 minutes.

5. Add coconut milk, salt, and tomato paste and simmer, uncovered, for an additional 30 minutes, until gravy is thick.

# Lamb/Mutton Curry *(Elu Mas Curry)*

*This dish can be made with either lamb or goat (mutton), which is a popular alternative to beef in a predominantly Buddhist and Hindu country like Sri Lanka.*

## Ingredients

- 2 pounds (1 kg) lamb or mutton, cut into 1-inch (2.5-cm) cubes
- 3 tablespoons roasted curry powder (page 41)
- 1 to 2 teaspoons cayenne pepper powder
- 1 teaspoon paprika
- 1 tablespoon apple cider vinegar
- 2 tablespoons oil
- 1 large onion, chopped
- 4 cloves garlic, chopped
- 2-inch (5-cm) piece ginger, chopped
- 2 green chilies, sliced
- 2-inch (5-cm) stalk lemongrass
- 2-inch (5-cm) cinnamon stick
- 1 sprig curry leaves
- 1½ cups (375 ml) water
- 1½ cups (375 ml) coconut milk
- 2 teaspoons salt
- 1 tablespoon tomato paste

Makes 6 servings

## Cooking Instructions

1. Prick meat all over with a fork to tenderize.

2. Slightly toast curry powder in a pan for 2 to 3 minutes. Mix with meat, cayenne powder, paprika, and vinegar and marinate for at least 1 to 2 hours (or overnight for optimum results).

3. Heat oil in pot. Sauté onions, garlic, ginger, green chilies, lemongrass, cinnamon stick, and curry leaves until onions are translucent.

4. Add marinated meat and stir-fry for a few minutes until browned.

5. Add water and bring to boil. Reduce heat, cover and simmer for 30 minutes.

6. Add coconut milk, salt, and tomato paste and simmer on low heat, uncovered, for an additional 30 minutes.

# Jaffna Goat Curry

*This Tamil version of goat curry kicks up the heat a few notches due to the addition of Jaffna curry powder and extra dry chilies. As goat tends to be tough, cooking it longer will help to tenderize the meat, as well as adding a pinch of baking powder to the gravy.*

## Ingredients

- *1 pound (454 g) goat meat, cut into 1-inch (2.5-cm) pieces*
- *1 tablespoon Jaffna curry powder (page 42)*
- *2 tablespoons oil*
- *1 onion, chopped*
- *2 dry red chilies, broken up*
- *1 sprig curry leaves*
- *½ teaspoon fennel seeds*
- *½ teaspoon mustard seeds*
- *1 cup (250 ml) water*
- *1 cup (250 ml) coconut milk*
- *salt to taste*
- *1 tablespoon tomato puree*

**Makes 4 to 6 servings**

## Cooking Instructions

**1.** Season goat meat with curry powder and set aside.

**2.** Heat oil in pan. Sauté onions, chilies, and curry leaves. As soon as onions are browned add fennel seeds and mustard seeds and sauté another minute.

**3.** Add the seasoned goat meat and stir-fry for 2 minutes until meat is browned.

**4.** Add water and bring to a boil. Cover, reduce heat and simmer for 30 minutes.

**5.** Add coconut milk, salt, and tomato puree and simmer, uncovered, an additional 30 minutes, until meat is tender and gravy is thick.

# Liver, Peas & Cashews in Curry

*This interesting combination dish is often served as an accompaniment to biryani. I use beef liver for this dish but feel free to use chicken livers if you prefer.*

## Ingredients

- ¼ *pound (113 g) raw cashew nuts*
- ½ *pound (226 g) beef liver*
- *2 teaspoons coriander powder*
- ½ *teaspoon cumin powder*
- ½ *to 1 teaspoon cayenne pepper powder*
- ½ *teaspoon ground black pepper*
- ½ *teaspoon apple cider vinegar*
- *2 tablespoons oil*
- *1 onion, chopped*
- *2 cloves garlic, sliced*
- *2 cardamom pods*
- *1-inch (2.5-cm) cinnamon stick*
- *1 sprig curry leaves*
- *1 cup (113 g) frozen peas*
- *1 cup (250 ml) coconut milk*
- *1¼ teaspoons salt*

**Makes 6 to 8 servings**

## Cooking Instructions

**1.** Soak cashews in water for 2 to 3 hours. Drain.

**2.** Wash liver and remove membrane. Cut into small pieces and mix with coriander powder, cumin powder, cayenne powder, black pepper, and vinegar. Allow to marinate for at least 30 minutes.

**3.** Heat oil in pan. Sauté onions, garlic, cardamom pods, cinnamon stick, and curry leaves until onions are translucent.

**4.** Add marinated liver and stir-fry for 5 minutes. Remove liver.

**5.** Add cashews, peas, coconut milk, and salt and simmer for 20 minutes. Add fried liver and cook an additional 5 minutes.

# Nimal's Deviled Meat

Deviled or "spiced" meats such as these are considered finger foods in Sri Lanka, and make the perfect hors d'oeuvre accompanied by a cold beer. This preparation, which includes soy sauce, is of Malay origin, but has truly become an island standard. Although there are infinite variations on the "deviled" theme, this recipe was given to me by Nimal, a former chef at the well-known Park View Lodge in Colombo.

## Ingredients

- 1 pound (454 g) boneless beef, chicken, or pork
- salt to taste
- black pepper to taste
- 1 to 2 teaspoons cayenne pepper powder
- 2 tablespoons soy sauce
- 3 tablespoons oil
- 1 onion, sliced
- 3 cloves garlic, sliced
- 2-inch (5-cm) piece ginger, sliced
- 2 Serrano chilies, sliced
- 1 tomato, diced
- 3 tablespoons tomato sauce
- 1 teaspoon sugar
- 1 teaspoon apple cider vinegar
- ½-inch (1.25-cm) cinnamon stick

**Makes 6 servings**

## Cooking Instructions

1. Slice meat into small chunks or strips. Season with salt, pepper, cayenne powder, and soy sauce, and marinate for at least 1 hour.

2. Heat oil in pan and stir-fry meat until cooked. Remove meat.

3. Add a little more oil and fry onions, garlic, ginger, chilies, and tomato.

4. Add tomato sauce, sugar, vinegar, and cinnamon stick.

5. Add meat back into pan and mix well. Stir-fry for an additional 5 minutes.

# Egg Curry

*This mild dish is usually a child's first curry, generally accompanied by plain rice.*

## Ingredients

- 4 hard-boiled eggs
- ¼ teaspoon turmeric powder
- 2 tablespoons oil
- 1 onion, chopped
- 3 cloves garlic, minced
- 1-inch (2.5-cm) piece ginger, sliced
- 2 green chilies, slit from base to stem
- 1-inch (2.5-cm) piece pandanus (optional)
- 1-inch (2.5-cm) stalk lemongrass
- 1-inch (2.5-cm) cinnamon stick
- 2 teaspoons raw curry powder (page 41)
- 1 sprig curry leaves
- 1 cup (250 ml) coconut milk
- salt to taste
- pinch saffron
- juice of 1 lime

## Cooking Instructions

**1.** Shell eggs. Prick with toothpick and rub with turmeric powder. Heat oil in pan. Fry whole eggs until golden brown on outside. Remove and set aside.

**2.** Fry onions, garlic, ginger, green chilies, pandanus, lemongrass, cinnamon stick, curry powder, and curry leaves until onions are translucent.

**3.** Add coconut milk, salt, and saffron and bring to a boil. Then reduce heat and simmer for 10 to 15 minutes.

**4.** Add eggs and cook for an additional 5 minutes.

**5.** Cool slightly and squeeze on lime juice. Mix well before serving.

**Makes 4 servings**

# Aunt Padma's Beef Smore

*This traditional version of pot roast, adapted from the Dutch, transforms into a uniquely Sri Lankan creation with the addition of lime pickle, chilies, coconut milk, and spices. An old-school dish that is not very popular today, this recipe comes from my Aunt Padma who considers it one of her specialties even though she is currently a vegetarian.*

## Ingredients

- *1 piece (3 to 4 pounds / 1.5 to 2 kgs) beef tenderloin*
- *1 tablespoon lime pickle*
- *2 tablespoons coriander powder*
- *1 tablespoon cayenne pepper powder*
- *½ teaspoon fenugreek seeds*
- *2 teaspoons cumin powder, roasted*
- *2 teaspoons fennel powder, roasted*
- *1 onion, chopped*
- *2 cloves garlic, chopped*
- *2-inch (5-cm) piece ginger, chopped*
- *1 sprig curry leaves*
- *2 cloves*
- *2-inch (5-cm) stalk lemongrass*
- *1-inch (2.5-cm) cinnamon stick*
- *3 tablespoons vinegar*
- *3 cups (750 ml) water*
- *1½ teaspoons salt*
- *1 cup (250 ml) coconut milk*
- *2 tablespoons oil*

## Cooking Instructions

1. Wash and dry meat. Remove all gristle. Prick with fork all over to tenderize or pound with meat hammer. Rub with lime pickle, coriander powder, cayenne powder, fenugreek seeds, cumin powder, and fennel powder. Marinate for at least 2 to 3 hours (or overnight for optimum results).

2. Add meat and all remaining ingredients except half the onions, coconut milk, and oil to a medium pot. Bring to a boil, then reduce heat and simmer, uncovered, until meat is tender and liquid has almost evaporated (about 1½ to 2 hours).

3. Add coconut milk and simmer for an additional 10 minutes. Remove meat and reserve gravy.

4. Heat oil in a separate pot and sauté reserved onions until golden brown. Add meat and brown on all sides.

5. Slice meat on a serving tray and pour reserved gravy over the meat.

> **Makes 4 to 6 servings**

# Duck Curry with Arrack *(Thara Curry)*

*Though not commonly eaten among the local populace, duck was a favorite of the British during the colonial era, and this seems like a dish made with them in mind. Arrack, the liquor of choice in Sri Lanka, distilled from the sap of the coconut palm flower, perfectly complements this rich dish. But if you can't find any, whiskey will do just fine.*

## Ingredients

- *2 tablespoons curry powder*
- *1 tablespoon cayenne pepper powder*
- *½ teaspoon ground black pepper*
- *1 whole duck, separated into joints*
- *juice of 1 lime*
- *3 tablespoons vinegar*
- *½ teaspoon turmeric powder*
- *salt to taste*
- *1 onion, chopped*
- *4 cloves garlic, chopped*
- *2-inch (5-cm) piece ginger, chopped*
- *1 sprig curry leaves*
- *2-inch (5-cm) piece pandanus (optional)*
- *2-inch (5-cm) stalk lemongrass*
- *2-inch (5-cm) cinnamon stick*
- *½ cup (125 ml) water*
- *1½ cups (375 ml) coconut milk*
- *1 tablespoon sugar*
- *¼ cup (65 ml) arrack or whiskey*

### For tempering:
- *2 tablespoons oil or ghee*
- *1 onion, chopped*
- *1 sprig curry leaves*

## Cooking Instructions

**1.** Slightly roast curry powder, cayenne powder, and ground black pepper.

**2.** Wash and cut duck into 3-inch pieces. Rub with lime juice, vinegar, turmeric powder, salt, and roasted spices. Marinate for at least 3 hours (or overnight for optimum results).

**3.** Place duck pieces in a medium pot with remaining ingredients except sugar, arrack, and tempering ingredients. Bring to a boil, then cover, reduce heat and simmer until duck is done (about 30 minutes).

**4.** Add sugar and arrack and cover and simmer for an additional 10 to 15 minutes. Remove duck and reserve gravy.

**5.** To temper, heat oil or ghee in a large frying pan and fry onions and curry leaves. Add duck pieces and brown. Add gravy and stir for 2 to 3 minutes.

**6.** Serve on a dish garnished with potato sticks.

Makes 6 servings

# Seafood

# Squid Curry *(Dhallo Curry)*

*Squid needs to be cooked either very quickly or for a very long time in order for it to be tender and not rubbery. This curried method is both quick and easy, and yields a delicious dish.*

## Ingredients

- 1 pound (454 g) squid
- 1 tablespoon roasted curry powder (page 41)
- 1 teaspoon fenugreek seeds
- 1 to 2 teaspoons cayenne pepper powder
- 2 tablespoons oil
- 1 onion, chopped
- 4 cloves garlic, ground
- 2-inch (5-cm) piece ginger, ground
- 2 to 3 green chilies, sliced
- 1 sprig curry leaves
- 1½ cups (375 ml) coconut milk
- salt to taste
- juice of 1 lime

Makes 6 servings

## Cooking Instructions

1. Wash, clean, and cut squid into 1-inch (2.5-cm) strips. Mix with curry powder, fenugreek seeds, and cayenne powder. Set aside.

2. Heat oil in pan. Fry onions until translucent. Add garlic, ginger, green chilies, and curry leaves.

3. Add squid and stir-fry for 2 minutes. Add coconut milk and salt and bring to a boil. Reduce heat and simmer for 5 minutes.

4. Cool slightly and stir in lime juice before serving.

# Leela

Leela has been a member of my family for the last 32 years, yet I know virtually nothing about her. She has been there through the death of my uncle and the birth of my cousin's two children. She has been there through richer and poorer, good times and bad, in sickness and in health. She never married, and no one—not even my 80-year-old Aunty Dora, her employer—knows exactly how old she is. She has just been there, as permanent a fixture as my aunt's blood red Peugeot 504 rusting in the garage, but now we have to take her back to her village.

I don't even think she really wants to go, but my aunt says it's high time. After all, Leela looks like she could use someone to take care of her now. Her face, wrinkled like a prune, and graying head of hair pulled back in a *konde* or bun only tell a portion of the story. Her hunched back makes her tiny four-foot frame appear even smaller. Her bunioned feet, with their permanently splayed-out toes resting sideways on the ground, could walk on broken glass and not feel a thing. But ever since she broke her hip a few years ago, she waddles more than walks. The injury was serious enough that my cousin Sam actually had to carry her to the bathroom every time she needed to use it for a while. It's a wonder she ever recovered at all considering the only treatment she received came at the hands of a local Ayurvedic practitioner or *wedemahathaya,* who applied a daily poultice of foul-smelling herbs (I might add though that this same remedy did the trick when I hurt my back earlier during my stay). These days, if there is no breakfast or tea to be made, errands to be run, or sweeping or washing up to be done, Leela can usually be found in her room napping or watching TV.

"Servants," as they are known in Sri Lanka, are hard to come by today, says my aunt, and good, loyal, trustworthy ones like Leela are a scarcity. After all, girls from the village can find better paying work as domestics in the Middle East, as long as they can get the necessary papers and an airline ticket. Today, overseas employment agencies specialize in this service, and people are lining up to sell themselves into indentured servitude. The TVs, gas cookers, and refrigerators—the spoils of their toils—that they bring back to their villages make it worth their while.

As the only member of my sizeable clan to have been born and raised in the U.S., I have always felt uncomfortable with the very concept of servants, though they are common in middle-class Colombo households. Even the word itself bothers me. But try as I may to take care of my own needs when I am visiting, Leela has always been there to wash my clothes, prepare my meals, run errands, and bring endless cups of iced coffee. She's taken care of me when I've been sick; spied and reported on me when I've been up to mischief; and taught me what little Sinhalese I know as she is the only member of the household who doesn't speak English. She's like a second mother, and except for my aunt, refers to everyone in the family—even my 55-year-old cousin Sam—as *baba* or "baby."

Leela was supposed to return to her village two years ago, but something always comes up. When the date was finally set for a weekend in April, the monsoons arrived early. "We'll have to wait until the rains let up," said Sam's wife, Charmalie. She works full-time in an office so Leela is especially a boon for her. When Leela leaves my aunt's family, who has depended on her for all these years, they will have to manage on their own. They found another girl, Iraesha, to come in and cook lunch during the week, but she will not live at the Park Street flat like Leela. Lee-

Leela with the author.

la's closet-like quarters off the kitchen will probably be converted into storage space or maybe a bedroom for Sam's teenage son Shanaka, who currently shares a room with his older sister Shalini. As Leela's departure kept being put off and put off, I never thought I'd actually see her go. Then one day my aunt gave the word, "We are taking Leela back on the last weekend in May."

Once the announcement was made, preparations slowly came together. There were personal possessions to pack up; fabrics to buy; certain appliances—like a new fan and radio—to procure; and even a gift of jewelry. Leela wanted a pair of nice gold earrings, and my aunt, usually the thrifty one, did not think twice about indulging her wishes as she might her own granddaughter. After all, she has known Leela longer than both her deceased husbands combined. Leela, who was previously employed by another of my aunts, has seen several generations of my family to adulthood. Bent and withered like an old but majestic Bo tree, this little lady is an institution, and her departure marks the end of an era.

When the appointed day arrived, I joined my aunt, my cousin, his wife and kids, their friend Kapu, and Premadasa, the driver, to see Leela off. We were taking her to her village outside the town of Chilaw, about 2½ hours north of Colombo, where her younger sister Karuna and her family own a small plot of land that they farm. Apparently, they have a river running through their back yard, and a small, spare room waiting for Leela. As Premadasa stuffed the back of the van to capacity with Leela's worldly possessions, which filled a motley assortment of bags and boxes, the rest of us gathered in the sitting room, sipping tea and eating fish buns. Despite the task ahead, the mood was light. After all, these city-dwellers rarely go "out-station," as the vast country outside the capital is commonly referred to, so the trip was as much a Saturday outing as it was about Leela retiring.

No one, including myself, had ever been to Chilaw, so that was cause for some excitement as well. This town, on the edge of a huge lagoon, was renowned for its seafood—especially humungous crabs, which

they make into a fiery crab curry. Chilaw crab curry is as well-known a regional dish in Sri Lanka as gumbo is in New Orleans, and a Cancer myself, I could not get enough of my fellow crabs simmering in a thick, spicy gravy, which Leela always prepared especially for me. When I realized that she was really leaving, and that her crab curry might become a lost art, I made sure to personally observe her preparing it one more time.

We used much smaller sea crabs this time, not the prized lagoon variety, which commanded prices as hefty as their size in places as far away as Singapore. Leela, like most Sri Lankan cooks, never measures, so I stood over her with a handy set of measuring spoons on a ring, and made her empty the contents of her hands into the spoons so I could faithfully capture the correct formula. After splitting the crabs in half (legs on) with her hands, and washing and cleaning the insides, she seasoned them with turmeric, chili powder, and a pinch of allspice. Then she turned her attention to a roasting pan, in which she placed some raw rice, peppercorns, and cumin seeds. When these were sufficiently browned she emptied the pan and roasted some freshly shredded coconut until it turned black. I could already tell she was going to use this as the base for the dark gravy for which crab curry is known.

In a pot big enough to hold all the crabs, she heated coconut oil, whose earthy aroma soon filled the small kitchen and, in fact, the whole Park Street flat. As soon as it started sizzling and smoking, she added chopped onions and tomatoes, curry leaves, a grass called rampe (pandanus), and an ingredient I was sure would not be available in the States, murungu leaves. Crab Curry is one of the few dishes that use these small, oval-shaped leaves, but my aunt assured me that it could be made without them. When the onions took on a translucent glow, Leela added the crabs and just enough water to cover the bottom of the pot, allowing them to steam with the lid on. Next she gathered the roasted ingredients on the granite grinding stone, which was almost as big as her. This apparent relic of the stone age still proves useful in the modern kitchen, I soon discovered, as she made quick work turning the rice, peppercorns, cumin, coconut, and fresh garlic into a dark paste that she added to the pot along with some coconut milk. After soaking some tamarind in a cup of water, she removed the seeds and fiber, leaving a rich juice, which she also added to the pot along with some salt. The crabs were done in no time, and the curry tasted as finger-licking good as it always did, leaving my mouth to burn in pleasure. If I accomplished nothing else on this trip at least I had preserved Leela's Chilaw crab curry recipe for posterity.

Packed up and ready to go, we piled into the family van, a lime green nine-seater. In lieu of SUVs, vans like these are actually very common on the bustling streets of Colombo as they run on cheaper diesel fuel. Carpooling also seems to be standard practice among adults and children alike here, though it hardly seems to limit the number of vehicles clogging up the roads. My aunt had already decided that the trip was too long for her to make, so we watched as she said goodbye to her trusted right hand, probably the only other person on the planet who had any inkling of what was stashed in her legendary *almirahs* (and, more importantly, exactly where it was

*Anthony Bourdain relaxes with the cook, Leela, after enjoying a meal at her house that was filmed for the Sri Lanka episode of Bourdain's popular Travel Channel series "No Reservations."*

stashed). Leela, whose eyes appeared as threatening as monsoons all morning, finally let loose a deluge of tears as my aunt sternly reprimanded, "What's this nonsense?"Aunty Dora has always been one tough cookie, but as the eldest of eight siblings, she's seen it, done it, and been through it all before. She is as thrifty with her emotions as she is with everything

else. Giving Leela a white lace handkerchief to mop up her face, she waved to us as we drove off.

Of course, Sri Lankans can never simply go from point A to point B. Only after making three different stops—for gas, batteries for the camera, and short-eats for the long ride—did we really hit the road. Then after about an hour or so, Shalini started feeling queasy, so we stopped for some roadside refreshments. Leela, adorned in a white cotton sari and spectacles, passively sipped her tea lost in thought. Leaving the family she had known for the last 32 years to rejoin her own blood relations, she must have been experiencing all sorts of bittersweet emotions in that moment, but when she caught my eyes she flashed her familiar, comforting smile.

The dusty two-lane blacktop that took us to Chilaw cut across lush green landscapes and skirted sandy, palm-studded coastline as it weaved through town after town. The absence of highways here makes any road trip a true adventure—the wind whipping through your hair as you pass an elephant effortlessly hauling timber with its serpentine trunk; a herd of grazing water buffalo; or fishermen perched on poles in the middle of the surf. Finally, we left the paved road behind for a dirt path that seemed to take us to the middle of the jungle. We had arrived in rural Sri Lanka, or the 'village,' as they call it, a glimpse of which you rarely get within the crowded confines of urban Colombo. Here trees outnumbered people and buildings, and life flowed with the rhythms of nature. Leela was returning to a simpler, less-complicated life and I, a refugee from the U.S., was envious.

When we pulled up to her sister's house I was surprised to see a very well-maintained plaster and brick dwelling at the end of the short driveway. The word "village" conjured up romantic notions of wood and mud huts in my mind, but Leela's people were obviously accustomed to far greater comfort. Three adorable girls of varying height but identical dress—blue hand-sewn frocks—bounced around barefoot on the veranda beaming brilliant smiles. Though they had not spent much time with their *Achi*, or great aunt, up till now, they were certainly looking forward to the chance to catch up. Leela's two grown nieces—the kids' mothers—and their mother Karuna, who looked even senior to her older sister, greeted their diminutive relation with a flurry of hugs and smiles. Happy to receive visitors as well in their solitary retreat, their smiles never faded over the course of the afternoon.

Hospitality stands as a hallmark of Sri Lankan culture, and no sooner were we out of the van than one of the little girls brought around a tray of cool drinks for everyone—passion fruit cordial, my favorite. Then Sam, Kapu, and I helped Premadasa unload Leela's belongings into her vacant room, a bright and airy improvement over her former digs (the adjoining bathroom itself was bigger than her old room in Colombo). Shanaka and Shalini went off to play with the little girls, while the women-folk retired to the kitchen at the back of the house where they had been busy preparing lunch.

Their traditional kitchen was actually nothing more than an open hearth whose fire crackled with the dried husks of coconut. Nothing went to waste here. Even coconut shells were made into bowls, spoons, or other implements. Over the open flames, a reddish-brown clay pot bubbled with an aromatic curry as Leela's nieces peeled and cut jackfruit, long beans, onions, and green chilies on bamboo mats on the dirt floor. There were no tables, chairs, counters, or even an oven, though a half-sized refrigerator shared space with a small sink in an adjoining annex.

The whole house itself was similarly appointed—three small bedrooms with only straw mats to sleep on and a central living room in which the only furniture consisted of some rattan chairs and a wooden table, on which rested a bulky TV set. Leela had brought a TV for her own room as well, and when the nieces' husbands arrived they spent the afternoon attaching a huge antennae to the roof of the house. True to its name, the outhouse sat several feet behind the kitchen, and consisted of nothing more than a concrete hole in the ground housed in a wooden booth.

I led the city slickers on an exploration of the immense grounds. What had seemed at first like unkempt jungle gave way to well-organized plots of cultivation containing every conceivable kind of fruit and vegetable. There were mango, papaya, and banana trees; cucumbers, gotu kola, pumpkin, beans, jackfruit, chilies, and coconut. I even saw my first cashew tree and picked and ate a red cashew fruit

*Leela's crab curry*

was the novelty of such a place that I found attractive or if I could really live here, away from the stress, savagery, and artificiality of modern life. Probably the latter.

By the time we emerged from the river, dried off in the sun, and made our way back to the house, lunch was ready. Clay pots containing various curries covered the small living room table. There was chicken curry, coconut sambol, cashew curry, jackfruit, rice, *paripoo* (lentils), and crispy papadum—most of which had been grown right there on the premises. This wholly organic meal, made from the natural bounty growing around us, tasted beyond amazing, and I would compare it to the best meals I've had in Sri Lanka. I washed it down with some fresh coconut toddy that Sam had got from just down the road from a man who climbed the tree right before his eyes to tap it. Toddy is the sap of the coconut flower, which when boiled down yields *pani*, a sweet, rich syrup. When fermented it makes arrack, the local coconut liquor. Though Chilaw crab curry was not on the menu, I could not be disappointed. At least I had the secret recipe now and could make it myself.

An inevitable outpouring of emotion coincided with our time of departure as Charmalie, Shanaka, Shalini, and Leela all broke down upon saying their last goodbyes. I was surprised that Sam, who has known Leela since his early 20s, didn't shed a tear, but then again, he is stoic like his mother. These people could and would, of course, visit Leela again. As for me, I didn't know when I would be coming back. Still, I was very happy for Leela when I said goodbye because I knew she was in good hands, among family, and in a peaceful and amazing place. I knew she wouldn't have to work anymore, but could now enjoy the company of her nieces and grandnieces. Of course, if she insisted on staying active there were plenty of chores to keep her busy. After a lifetime of service to others, I think Leela deserved to begin this new chapter in her life. After crouching down and giving her a big bear hug for the last time, I departed with a smile. ❖

right from its slender branches. Cashew nuts, as Sam informed me, came from another part of the tree and must be carefully harvested to prevent being burned by their acid-laced covering. By this time the girls and their white dog Harry had joined the trek, escorting us to the back of the property, where, sure enough, we stumbled upon a peaceful meandering river.

Harry needed no invitation to dart into the water followed by the girls, fully clothed and laughing, in what must have been a daily ritual. A bit further downstream, women scrubbed and slapped clothes clean against the rocks as a swarm of young boys played an impromptu game of cricket partly in the shallow river itself. As the midday heat was clawing, the rest of us decided to go for a dip as well. Since it was not very deep, it was better to float on your back or paddle than try to wade through the stony riverbed, which was hard on the soles of your feet. Immersed in cool water, beneath blue skies, and surrounded by nature's fullness, I could not imagine a more idyllic setting. I wondered to myself whether it

# Leela's Chilaw Crab Curry *(Kakuluwo Curry)*

*Leela, my Aunt Dora's maid for some 32 years, hails from the town of Chilaw on Sri Lanka's west coast, a place famous for its lagoons as well as a fiery crab curry. Not many members of my family can eat food this hot so I usually end up eating the whole dish myself. Of course, for a more moderate version, take it easy on the cayenne pepper powder.*

## Ingredients

- 5 large crabs
- ½ teaspoon turmeric powder
- I to 2 tablespoons cayenne pepper powder
- ¼ teaspoon ground allspice
- about I teaspoon salt (to taste)
- I tablespoon raw rice
- ½ teaspoon black peppercorns
- I teaspoon cumin seeds
- 3 tablespoons shredded coconut
- 5 cloves garlic
- 2 tablespoons oil
- I onion, chopped
- I sprig curry leaves
- I tomato, chopped
- 2-inch (5-cm) piece pandanus (optional)
- I bunch murungu leaves (optional)
- I cup (250 ml) water
- I cup (250 ml) coconut milk
- 2 tablespoons tamarind fruit, soaked in ¼ cup (65 ml) water

## Cooking Instructions

1. Wash and clean crabs (remove gills and dirt). Split down the middle and crack legs so gravy can penetrate.

2. Toss crabs with turmeric powder, cayenne powder, allspice, and salt. Set aside.

3. Roast rice, peppercorns, and cumin seeds together. Then roast coconut until brown. Grind these ingredients with garlic and set aside.

4. Heat oil in medium pot. Sauté onions, curry leaves, tomato, pandanus, and murungu leaves.

5. Add crabs and ½ cup of the water. Cover and steam over high heat for 15 minutes.

6. Combine rice mixture with the remaining water and coconut milk and add to pot. Stir and simmer for 10 minutes.

7. Strain seeds from soaked tamarind and add liquid to pot. Simmer an additional 5 minutes. The gravy should be dark and rich.

**Makes 4 to 6 servings**

# Deviled Shrimp or Squid

*More like a Chinese stir-fry than a Sri Lankan curry, this dish makes for quick, convenient finger food, and a perfect accompaniment for a cold beer.*

## Ingredients

- *1 pound (454 g) shrimp or squid*
- *2 tablespoons oil*
- *1 onion, sliced*
- *4 cloves garlic, sliced*
- *1 teaspoon crushed ginger*
- *1 sprig curry leaves*
- *2 medium tomatoes, peeled and diced*
- *4 Serrano chilies, sliced diagonally*
- *1 teaspoon cayenne pepper powder*
- *2 dry red chilies, crushed*
- *2 tablespoons apple cider vinegar*
- *salt to taste*
- *juice of 1 lime*

**Makes 4 to 6 servings**

## Cooking Instructions

1. Wash, clean, and shell shrimp or cut squid into 1-inch (2.5-cm) strips.

2. Heat oil in pan. Sauté onions, garlic, ginger, and curry leaves until onions are translucent. Add tomatoes and Serrano chilies.

3. Add shrimp or squid, cayenne powder, dry red chilies, vinegar, and salt and stir-fry for 2 minutes.

4. Remove from heat, put on a plate, and squeeze on lime juice before serving.

# Shrimp Curry *(Isso Curry)*

*The year-round availability of shrimp or prawns makes this a popular dish in Sri Lanka. It also happens to be one of my favorites because of the complexity of flavors from spicy to tangy (notably with the addition of tamarind).*

## Ingredients

- *1 pound (454 g) shrimp*
- *2 tablespoons roasted curry powder (page 41)*
- *1 to 2 teaspoons cayenne pepper powder*
- *¼ teaspoon fenugreek seeds*
- *2 tablespoons oil*
- *1 onion, chopped*
- *1 tablespoon crushed ginger*
- *4 cloves garlic, chopped*
- *2 to 3 green chilies, chopped*
- *1 sprig curry leaves*
- *1-inch (2.5-cm) piece pandanus (optional)*
- *1-inch (2.5-cm) stalk lemongrass*
- *1-inch (2.5-cm) cinnamon stick*
- *1 cup (250 ml) coconut milk*
- *salt to taste*
- *1 tablespoon tamarind pulp, dissolved in ¼ cup (65 ml) warm water*
- *juice of 1 lime*

## Cooking Instructions

1. Wash, shell, and devein shrimp.
2. Slightly roast curry powder, cayenne powder, and fenugreek seeds for 2 minutes. Toss shrimp with spice mixture and set aside for 30 minutes.
3. Heat oil in pan. Sauté onions, ginger, garlic, green chilies, curry leaves, pandanus, lemongrass, and cinnamon stick until onions are translucent.
4. Add shrimp and stir-fry with other ingredients for 2 minutes.
5. Add coconut milk, salt, and tamarind solution and simmer just until shrimp turn red. DO NOT OVERCOOK.
6. Squeeze lime juice over shrimp before serving.

> **Makes 4 to 6 servings**

# Red Fish Curry *(Miris Malu)*

*As "red" in the name implies, the heavy dose of cayenne pepper powder puts this dish on the spicier side of the spectrum. For a less spicy version, use only a teaspoon of cayenne pepper powder. I recommend using tuna steaks for this dish, but use whatever firm-fleshed fish you prefer.*

## Ingredients

- 2 pounds (1 kg) fish steaks
- 1 tablespoon tamarind, soaked in ¼ cup (65 ml) warm water and seeds and fiber discarded*
- 2 tablespoons roasted curry powder (page 41)
- 1 to 2 teaspoons cayenne pepper powder
- ¼ teaspoon fenugreek seeds
- 1 teaspoon paprika
- 2 tablespoons oil
- 1 onion, sliced
- 2-inch (5-cm) piece ginger, sliced
- 3 cloves garlic, sliced
- 2 to 3 green chilies, slit from stem to tip
- 1 sprig curry leaves
- 1½ cups (325 ml) water
- 1½ teaspoons salt

## Cooking Instructions

**1.** Wash fish and cut into 1-inch (2.5-cm) chunks, removing any skin and bones.

**2.** Marinate fish in a mixture of the tamarind water, curry powder, cayenne powder, fenugreek seeds, and paprika for 30 minutes.

**3.** Heat oil in pan. Sauté onions, ginger, garlic, green chilies, and curry leaves until onions are translucent.

**4.** Add fish to pan with water and salt. Bring to a boil and then reduce heat and simmer, uncovered, for 10 to 15 minutes until fish is cooked.

*Tamarind paste or concentrate may be used, but maybe only ½ teaspoon, due to its intense flavor.

Makes 6 to 8 servings

# White Fish Curry *(Malu Kirata)*

*This curry is a much milder coconut milk-based dish popular among children. In fact, it is one of the first curries fed to toddlers. Kingfish or mackerel work really well in this dish.*

## Ingredients

- 2 pounds (1 kg) white fish steaks or fillets
- juice of 1 lime
- 1½ teaspoons salt
- ⅛ teaspoon turmeric powder
- 2 tablespoons oil
- 1 onion, sliced
- 3 cloves garlic, sliced
- 2 to 3 green chilies, chopped
- 1 sprig curry leaves
- 1 cup (250 ml) coconut milk
- ½ cup (125 ml) water
- 2-inch (5-cm) cinnamon stick
- 2-inch (5-cm) stalk lemongrass
- ¼ teaspoon fenugreek seeds

## Cooking Instructions

1. Wash and cut fish into 1-inch chunks, removing any skin and bones. Rub with lime juice, salt, and turmeric powder and set aside.

2. Heat oil in pan. Sauté onions, garlic, green chilies, and curry leaves until onions are translucent.

3. Add fish, coconut milk, water, cinnamon stick, lemongrass, and fenugreek seeds.

4. Bring to a boil, then reduce heat and simmer for 7 to 8 minutes until fish is cooked

**Makes 6 to 8 servings**

# Fish Mustard Curry *(Abba Kiri Malu)*

*Mustard adds a spicy, tangy note to this popular fish dish.*

## Ingredients

- 1 pound (454 g) white fish steaks or fillets
- 2 tablespoons oil
- 1 onion, sliced
- 3 Serrano chilies or 1 green pepper, sliced into rings
- 1-inch (2.5-cm) cinnamon stick
- 2-inch (5-cm) stalk lemongrass
- 5 cloves
- 1 sprig curry leaves
- ½ cup (125 ml) water
- ½ cup (125 ml) coconut milk
- ¼ teaspoon turmeric powder
- 1 teaspoon salt
- juice of 1 lime

### Spice Paste:
- 1½ teaspoons brown mustard seeds
- ¼ teaspoon ground black pepper
- ½ teaspoon fennel seeds
- 2 cloves garlic
- 2-inch (5-cm) piece ginger
- ½ tablespoon shredded coconut
- 1 tablespoon vinegar
- ½ teaspoon sugar

## Cooking Instructions

**1.** Wash and cut fish into 1-inch chunks, removing any skin and bones.

**2.** Grind spice paste ingredients together in a food processor or blender. Rub into fish and set aside for 30 minutes.

**3.** Heat oil in pan. Sauté onions, chilies, cinnamon stick, lemongrass, cloves, and curry leaves until onion is translucent.

**4.** Add fish and toss for 2 minutes. Add water. Bring to a boil, then reduce heat and simmer for 5 to 7 minutes.

**5.** Add coconut milk, turmeric powder, and salt and simmer for an additional 5 minutes.

**6.** Squeeze on juice of lime before serving.

---

**Makes 4 to 6 servings**

# Sour Fish Curry *(Fish Ambul Thial)*

*This amazing dish, a remnant from the days of no refrigeration, only gets better with age. Goraka, an orange fruit that turns into a black, kidney-shaped node when dried, provides the tart taste while also acting as an excellent preservative. My grandmother loved to make this dish and so do I because of its complex levels of flavor.*

## Ingredients

- *1 pound (454 g) tuna steak*
- *5 cloves garlic, minced*
- *2-inch (5-cm) piece ginger, sliced*
- *½ teaspoon ground black pepper*
- *1 teaspoon fenugreek seeds*
- *5 pieces goraka (or 2 tablespoons tamarind pulp, soaked in ¼ cup warm water, with fiber and seeds removed)*
- *2 teaspoons salt*
- *2 tablespoons oil*
- *1 onion, finely chopped*
- *1 clove*
- *1 cardamom pod*
- *1-inch (2.5-cm) cinnamon stick*
- *1 sprig curry leaves*
- *2 green chilies, sliced*
- *½ cup (125 ml) water*

### Spice Blend:
- *2 teaspoons cayenne pepper powder*
- *½ teaspoon cumin powder*
- *½ teaspoon fennel powder*
- *1 teaspoon coriander powder*

## Cooking Instructions

**1.** Wash fish and cut into 1-inch cubes, removing any skin and bones.

**2.** Roast the spice blend ingredients in a small pan until fragrant. DO NOT BURN.

**3.** Place roasted spice blend, garlic, ginger, black pepper, fenugreek seeds, goraka or tamarind, and salt in a food processor and grind to a thick paste, adding a little water if necessary. Marinate fish in this mixture for 30 minutes.

**4.** Heat oil in a pan. Sauté onions, clove, cardamom pod, cinnamon stick, curry leaves, and green chilies until onions are translucent.

**5.** Add fish to pan with water and bring to a boil. Reduce heat and simmer until all water has evaporated. (Note: This is a dry curry with little or no gravy.)

| Makes 6 servings |
| --- |

# Shark Curry *(Mora Kalupol)*

*Shark is a meaty fish that soaks up the flavors of the ingredients well.* Kalupol *refers to a preparation that uses roasted shredded coconut to make a thick base for the gravy.*

## Ingredients

- 1 pound (454 g) shark steak
- 3 tablespoons shredded coconut
- 1 to 2 teaspoons cayenne pepper powder
- 2 teaspoons cumin powder
- 2 teaspoons coriander powder
- 1/2 teaspoon fennel powder
- 2 pieces goraka (or 1 tablespoon tamarind pulp, soaked in warm water, with fiber and seeds removed)
- 3 cloves garlic, finely chopped
- 2-inch (5-cm) piece ginger, finely chopped
- 2 tablespoons oil
- 1/2 inch (1.25-cm) cinnamon stick
- 1/4 cup (65 ml) water
- salt to taste

## Cooking Instructions

1. Cut shark into 1-inch cubes, removing any skin and bones.

2. Roast coconut with powdered spices until browned.

3. Soak goraka in boiling water and grind to a paste.

4. Combine dry-roasted ingredients with goraka, garlic, and ginger in a food processor to make a thick paste. Coat fish well with the paste and set aside to marinate for about 30 minutes.

5. Heat oil in pan. Add fish and cinnamon stick and stir-fry for 2 to 3 minutes.

6. Add water and salt and bring to a boil. Then reduce heat and simmer about 20 to 25 minutes.

**Makes 4 to 6 servings**

# Vegetables, Legumes, Fruits & Nuts

*S*ri Lankans consume prodigious amounts of fresh fruits and vegetables as part of their daily diet, many of which are not even known or available in the west. From fleshy jackfruit to mineral-packed gotu kola leaves, and even crunchy lotus root, many unique offerings abound on the Sri Lankan dinner table. A rice and curry meal invariably features several vegetables to complement one or two meat or fish curries. Generally vegetable curries use the raw curry powder—not roasted—for a much milder flavor.

# Sri Lankan Lentils *(Paripoo)*

*No Sri Lankan meal would be complete without these high-protein legumes, which soak up the flavors of coconut milk, lemongrass, and cinnamon. When eaten with rice, they comprise a perfect protein. You can vary the consistency of the lentils, or dhal, as they are known in both Sri Lanka and India, from thick as oatmeal to watery as soup, depending on how much liquid you add.*

## Ingredients

- ½ pound (226 g) lentils
- 2 cups (500 ml) water
- ½ onion, chopped
- 2 to 3 green chilies, sliced
- 2 cloves garlic, sliced
- 1-inch (2.5-cm) piece pandanus (optional)
- 1-inch (2.5-cm) stalk lemongrass
- 1-inch (2.5-cm) cinnamon stick
- 1 cardamom pod
- 1 clove
- ½ teaspoon turmeric powder
- ½ cup (125 ml) coconut milk
- salt to taste

### For tempering:
- 2 tablespoons oil
- ½ onion, sliced
- 1 sprig curry leaves
- 1 teaspoon black mustard seeds
- 2 whole dry red chilies

## Cooking Instructions

**1.** Wash and drain lentils, removing any stones or chaff.

**2.** Bring water to a boil in a medium-size pot. Add lentils, onion, green chilies, garlic, pandanus, lemongrass, cinnamon stick, cardamom pod, clove, and turmeric. Cover and simmer until lentils are soft (about 20 minutes).

**3.** Add coconut milk and salt. Cook for an additional 5 minutes stirring occasionally.

**4.** In another pan, heat tempering oil. Sauté onions and curry leaves until onions are translucent. Add mustard seeds and dry chilies. Fry until mustard seeds start to pop. Pour over lentils and mix well.

> **Makes 4 to 6 servings**

# A Trip to a Sri Lankan Market

Sri Lanka certainly boasts its fair share of modern supermarkets—namely the island-wide chains Keel's and Cargill's Food City. Though nothing on par with the lavish, über-stocked mega-markets of the U.S., they still offer some semblance of western-style food shopping in a familiar setting. But to really get a taste of how most of the local populace goes grocery shopping, you need go no further than any main street. The bustling capital of Colombo abounds with all manner of street vendors, sometimes peddling their wares on nothing more than a sackcloth laid out on the pavement. Since these vendors tend to congregate next to each other, usually around the busier thoroughfares, you find dozens of impromptu street markets. Additionally, several long-established covered markets around town featuring semi-permanent stalls offer a farmers' market feel with fresh, seasonal produce to match. No imported Peruvian asparagus or oranges from South Africa here, but rather mountains of local mangoes or pyramids of pineapple stacked neatly next to more obscure fruits and vegetables. In Sri Lanka, "local"

**Plantains**

and "sustainable" are not buzzwords but business as usual.

The best part about shopping at such open-air markets is being able to see, smell, touch, and taste the food you are eventually going to ingest. Bargaining is welcomed, but hardly necessary considering the comparatively low prices. I would feel bad trying to pay anything less than 50 cents for a plump, juicy pineapple. However, I do take full advantage of the opportunity to enjoy a whole host of foods I would never be able to find back in America—stuff like gotu kola, jackfruit, and rambutan. Gotu kola, a green plant with long stalks and rounded leaves, somewhat akin to cilantro, is typically used in *mallun* (a concoction that includes shredded coconut, lime juice, green chilies, and spices, page 135), a great side dish for rice and curry. Speaking of curries, *polos*, or young jackfruit is a personal favorite—probably because I'm only able to eat it in Sri Lanka. The oblong-shaped jackfruit, green in appearance and covered with hard "scales," is the largest tree-borne fruit in the world, sometimes reaching 80 pounds in weight, up to 36

*Rambutan*

inches in length, and 20 inches in diameter. It tastes like a cross between a potato and a plantain, and if it were up to me I would classify it as a vegetable.

As far as fruits go, I gorge myself on mangoes, papayas, pineapple, and plantain, but rambutan ranks as a childhood favorite. Certainly unique in appearance, their bright red hue and soft but spiny skin has earned them the nickname "hairy balls" in my family. Peeling off this outer layer reveals a sweet, tender white core that resembles a lichi fruit and tastes divine. While all of this produce may not be "certified organic" according to western standards, most small farmers who peddle their crops cannot afford expensive chemical fertilizers and pest protection. As a result, fruits and vegetables in Sri Lanka taste how they should taste, and not like flavorless facsimiles.

In addition to produce, meat and fish are also sold at street markets. But unlike the sanitized supermarket versions—in shrink-wrap and styrofoam—you see exactly where your food was sourced (in fact, maybe more than you wanted to see). Typically, freshly gutted carcasses—whether cow, pig, lamb, goat, or chicken—are hung up in the open air without refrigeration and with no protection from the flies, heat, and dust. Squawking crows congregate greedily waiting for a scrap, but nothing goes to

waste as all parts of the animals (including the offal) are for sale. *Barbath,* or cow's stomach, is a real delicacy here. Even the fish and seafood are not iced. The best they can hope for is a dousing of cold water to prevent them from drying out in the sun. But all of these animals have been killed or caught on the very same day they go to market, and they will be cooked and usually eaten on that same day as well. Despite having refrigeration at home, Sri Lankans prize fresh food and will make daily trips to the market because old habits die hard.

For the uninitiated, a trip to a Sri Lankan street market offers an eye opening, albeit sometimes scary, experience. Regardless, the sights, sounds, tastes, and people provide an excellent way to get to the heart of this culture (or any other for that matter). Though the absence of health codes, handling regulations, and plastic may make you feel as if you were taking your life into your hands, the simple fact is that people have been living this way for thousands of years without issue. The tainted food that prompts recalls—a symptom of our modern mass agricultural methods in the west—have never occurred in Sri Lanka. In fact, on my many trips there over the years, I can honestly say that food poisoning has never been an issue, only overindulgence! ✢

# Carrot Curry *(Karat Kirata)*

*This attractive dish adds color to a rice and curry menu.*

## Ingredients

- *1 pound (454 g) carrots*
- *2 tablespoons oil*
- *1 onion, chopped*
- *2 to 3 green chilies, chopped*
- *1 sprig curry leaves*
- *1 tablespoon raw curry powder (page 41)*
- *1 dry red chili, chopped*
- *1 teaspoon Maldive fish (or 1 tablespoon dry shrimp from any Asian market)*
- *½ teaspoon fenugreek seeds*
- *¼ teaspoon turmeric powder*
- *1 cup (250 ml) coconut milk*
- *salt to taste*

## Cooking Instructions

**1.** Wash, peel, and cut carrots into thin strips about an inch long.

**2.** Heat oil in pan. Sauté onions, green chilies, and curry leaves until onions are translucent.

**3.** Add carrots, curry powder, red chili, Maldive fish or dry shrimp, fenugreek seeds, and turmeric and toss for a few minutes.

**4.** Add coconut milk and salt and simmer for about 20 minutes until carrots are tender

**Makes 4 to 6 servings**

# Beetroot Curry *(Ratu Ala Curry)*

*This healthy and hearty root vegetable makes for a robust and attractive curry. Sri Lankans like to cook up the mineral rich beet leaves as well in a* mallun.

## Ingredients

- *1 pound (454 g) beets*
- *2 tablespoons oil*
- *1 onion, sliced*
- *1 sprig curry leaves*
- *2 to 3 green chilies, sliced*
- *3 teaspoons vinegar*
- *1 tablespoon raw curry powder (page 41)*
- *1 to 2 teaspoons cayenne pepper powder*
- *1 cup (250 ml) coconut milk*
- *salt to taste*

## Cooking Instructions

**1.** Peel beets and cut into thin strips about 1-inch (2.5-cm) long.

**2.** Heat oil in pan. Fry onions, curry leaves, and green chilies until onions are translucent.

**3.** Add beets, vinegar, curry powder, and cayenne powder. Mix well.

**4.** Add coconut milk and salt and simmer until beets are tender, about 20 to 30 minutes.

**Makes 4 to 6 servings**

# Potato Curry *(Ala Curry)*

*This very mild curry is popular among children. It adds just the right balance to a meal filled with spicier fare.*

## Ingredients

- 2 pounds (1 kg) potatoes
- 1 onion, sliced
- 2 to 3 green chilies, sliced
- 1 sprig curry leaves
- ¾ teaspoon fenugreek seeds
- ¾ teaspoon turmeric powder
- 1½ cups (375 ml) water
- ½ cup (125 ml) coconut milk
- salt to taste

## Cooking Instructions

1. Wash, peel, and dice potatoes.

2. Place all ingredients except coconut milk and salt into a pan and bring to a boil. Reduce heat and simmer until potatoes are soft, about 15 to 20 minutes.

3. Add coconut milk and salt and simmer an additional 5 minutes.

**Makes 4 to 6 servings**

# Spinach Curry *(Nivithi Curry)*

*Rich in iron and minerals, this curry may be eaten by itself or combined with lentils for a simple and healthy accompaniment to plain rice.*

## Ingredients

- 1 pound (454 g) spinach
- 1 onion, sliced
- 2 cloves garlic, sliced
- 2 to 3 green chilies, sliced
- 1 sprig curry leaves
- 1 tablespoon coriander powder
- ¼ teaspoon turmeric powder
- ¼ cup (65 ml) water
- ¼ cup (65 ml) coconut milk
- salt to taste

## Cooking Instructions

**1.** Wash and chop spinach.

**2.** Place all ingredients into a pan and cook on low heat for about 5 minutes. Toss well.

**Makes 4 to 6 servings**

# Sautéed Greens *(Mallun)*

*For this quick and simple way to prepare tasty greens, you may use kale, kohlrabi, mustard greens, turnip greens, collards, or whatever you like. I prefer kale myself.*

## Ingredients

- *1 bunch greens, finely chopped*
- *1 tablespoon oil*
- *1 onion, sliced*
- *½ teaspoon black mustard seeds*
- *2 to 3 tablespoons shredded coconut, fresh or desiccated (unsweetened)*
- *¼ teaspoon turmeric powder*
- *salt to taste*
- *juice of 1 lime*

## Cooking Instructions

1. Wash and dry greens. Finely chop or shred.

2. Heat oil in pan and sauté onions until translucent. Add mustard seeds and cook for 1 minute until they begin to pop.

3. Add greens, coconut, turmeric powder, and salt, and toss with a little water. Cook for 2 to 3 minutes. Squeeze lime juice over and mix well.

**Makes 4 to 6 servings**

# French Bean Curry *(Bonchi Curry)*

*This very mild "curry" would not be out of place on a menu consisting of Western dishes. In Sri Lanka they actually use long beans to make it, which you can find at any Asian store.*

## Ingredients

- *1 pound (454 g) French green beans, (haricot vert)*
- *2 tablespoons oil*
- *1 onion, sliced*
- *2 to 3 green chilies, sliced*
- *1 sprig curry leaves*
- *1 tablespoon raw curry powder (page 41)*
- *¼ teaspoon turmeric powder*
- *½ cup (125 ml) coconut milk*
- *½ cup (125 ml) water*
- *salt to taste*

**Makes 4 to 6 servings**

## Cooking Instructions

**1.** Wash and slice beans diagonally into 2-inch pieces.

**2.** Heat oil in pan. Sauté onions, green chilies, and curry leaves until onions are translucent.

**3.** Add raw curry powder and sauté for a minute. Add beans, turmeric powder, coconut milk, water, and salt.

**4.** Simmer, uncovered, for about 30 minutes until beans are tender and most of the liquid has evaporated.

# Cashew Nut Curry *(Cadju Curry)*

*Though plentiful on Sri Lanka, cashews are very labor intensive to harvest because they contain a poisonous sap. This makes them expensive and somewhat of a luxury food. This signature dish of Sri Lankan cuisine is often served to Buddhist monks at almsgivings or at other special occasions.*

## Ingredients

- ½ pound (226 g) raw cashew nuts
- 1½ cups (375 ml) water
- ½ teaspoon turmeric powder
- 1 teaspoon ghee
- 1 onion, chopped
- 2 cloves garlic, chopped
- 2-inch (5-cm) piece ginger, chopped
- 2-inch (5-cm) stalk lemongrass
- 2 to 3 green chilies, sliced
- 1 sprig curry leaves
- 1 tablespoon coriander powder
- 1 cup (250 ml) coconut milk
- salt to taste

**Makes 4 to 6 servings**

## Cooking Instructions

1. Soak cashews in water to cover overnight (ideally changing water a couple of times).

2. Drain nuts and boil in the 1½ cups water mixed with turmeric powder until tender. Drain.

3. Heat ghee in a pan. Fry onions, garlic, ginger, lemongrass, green chilies, and curry leaves until onions are translucent.

4. Add coriander powder, coconut milk, salt, and cooked cashews.

5. Cook on medium heat until liquid has almost evaporated.

# Moong Bean Curry *(Moong Ata)*

*A legume like lentils, moong beans offer an alternative to dhal. Popular in rural areas, this dish is an excellent source of proteins, vitamins, and minerals.*

## Ingredients

- 8 ounces (226 g) dry moong beans
- 2 tablespoons oil
- 1 onion, chopped
- 2 to 3 green chilies, chopped
- 1 sprig curry leaves
- 1 to 2 teaspoons cayenne pepper powder
- ½ teaspoon cumin powder
- ¼ teaspoon turmeric powder
- 1 cup (250 ml) coconut milk
- ½ cup (125 ml) water
- salt to taste

## Cooking Instructions

**1.** Soak beans overnight in water to cover. Drain.

**2.** Heat oil in pan. Sauté onions, green chilies, and curry leaves until onions are translucent.

**3.** Add powdered spices and stir for a minute.

**4.** Add moong beans, coconut milk, water, and salt. Bring to a boil, then reduce heat and simmer until beans are tender (about 30 minutes).

---

**Makes 4 to 6 servings**

# Lampreis

**L**ampreis has got to be one of my favorite Sri Lankan meals, distilling the island's cuisine down to its bare essence. Its nuance and complexity, however, are masked by its simplicity, since at face value it is nothing more than a bundle of rice and curry wrapped up in a banana leaf. In fact, the name itself comes from the Dutch, literally meaning "lump of rice," but I doubt you'll find anything remotely like this in Holland or anywhere else for that matter (while the origins of the dish can be traced to Indonesia, it probably arrived in Sri Lanka through indentured servants brought by the Dutch). When it comes to rice and curry, *lampreis* assumes its place at the pinnacle.

While purists argue about what exactly constitutes *lampreis*, after a lifetime of research, I have reached the conclusion that this meal must include the following components: samba rice cooked in a rich marrow bone stock; tempered *brinjal* (eggplant) curry; a cutlet or *frikadel;* a mixed meat curry of pork, beef, and mutton; *seeni* (sugar) *sambol;* fried ash plantain curry; and *blachan* (a condiment of Indonesian origin made of dried prawns, onions, salt, lime, and spices all ground together into a paste). Prepared individually, these dishes are then assembled together in a banana leaf and steamed so that the flavors meld together creating a rich and flavorful meal that is miles from the run-of-the-mill rice packet that Sri Lankans favor as a portable lunch. Whether it's the earthy flavor of the banana leaf that gives it that added edge or the interplay of the individual dishes themselves, to know *lampreis* is to love it.

In Sri Lanka today, many banana-leaf wrapped bundles masquerade as lampreis, but the best commercially available product can be found at three places—the esteemed Green Cabin eatery on Galle Road, a Colombo institution; The Fab, a newish bakery chain whose flagship store is in Colpetty; and of course, the Dutch Burgher Union, a members only club that thankfully sells its *lampreis* at a take-out counter at the back. I say commercially available because if you are lucky to know home cooks like Jean Daniels or Lorraine Bartholowmewz, who fill private bulk orders, you are in for the best, most authentic *lampreis* that money can buy. ✤

# Aunty Manel's Special Eggplant Curry (Vambotu Curry)

This is probably the tastiest preparation of eggplant that you will ever eat. Though the deep-frying makes it a little labor intensive, the final outcome justifies the extra effort. I could never get this dish quite right until my Aunty Manel gave me her recipe.

## Ingredients

- 1 pound (454 g) eggplant
- 1/4 teaspoon turmeric powder
- oil for deep-frying
- 3 cloves garlic
- 2-inch (5-cm) piece ginger
- 1 teaspoon sugar
- 1 teaspoon salt
- 1 tablespoon apple cider vinegar
- 1/2 cup (125 ml) water
- 2 tablespoons oil
- 1 onion, sliced
- 2 to 3 green chilies, sliced
- 1 sprig curry leaves
- 2-inch (5-cm) cinnamon stick
- 3 cloves
- 1 tablespoon raw curry powder (page 41)
- 1 to 2 teaspoons cayenne pepper powder
- 1 teaspoon brown mustard seeds, ground
- 1/2 cup (125 ml) coconut milk
- salt to taste

## Cooking Instructions

1. Wash eggplant and cut into 2-inch (5-cm) strips. Rub with salt and a dash of turmeric powder.

2. Deep fry eggplant until golden brown. Drain on newspaper.

3. Blend garlic, ginger, sugar, salt, apple cider vinegar, and water in a food processor to form a paste.

4. Heat the 2 tablespoons oil in pan. Sauté onions, green chilies, and curry leaves until onions are translucent. Add cinnamon stick, cloves, curry powder, cayenne powder, and ground mustard seeds.

5. Add blended garlic-ginger mixture and bring to a boil. Reduce heat and add fried eggplant, coconut milk, and salt. Toss well and simmer for 3 to 5 minutes.

Makes 4 to 6 servings

# Okra Curry *(Bandakka Curry)*

*Okra is a popular vegetable in Sri Lanka. Preparing it in this manner minimizes the stickiness, but make sure it is well stir-fried before adding the liquids.*

## Ingredients

- *1 pound (454 g) okra*
- *2 tablespoons oil*
- *1 onion, sliced*
- *2 to 3 green chilies, sliced*
- *1 sprig curry leaves*
- *¼ teaspoon turmeric powder*
- *½ teaspoon fenugreek seeds*
- *1 tablespoon coriander powder*
- *1 cup (250 ml) coconut milk*
- *¼ cup (65 ml) water*
- *salt to taste*

**Makes 4 to 6 servings**

## Cooking Instructions

**1.** Wash okra, cut off tops, and slice diagonally into 1-inch (2.5-cm) pieces.

**2.** Heat oil in pan. Sauté onions until translucent. Add green chilies, curry leaves, and okra and stir-fry for 2 to 3 minutes.

**3.** Add turmeric, fenugreek seeds, and coriander powder and toss well.

**4.** Add coconut milk, water, and salt and simmer until okra is tender, about 20 minutes.

# Spiced Potatoes *(Ala Thel Dala)*

*A dish that completes any menu, spiced potatoes is one of the most popular dishes in Sri Lanka. It is well worth the effort to find some Maldive fish, which in addition to its unique flavor, adds a nice chewy textural counterpoint to the tender potatoes.*

## Ingredients

- *1 large potato, peeled and diced*
- *2 tablespoons oil*
- *1 onion, sliced*
- *1 sprig curry leaves*
- *2 dry red chilies, ground (or 1 to 2 teaspoons red pepper flakes)*
- *1 teaspoon Maldive fish (optional)*
- *¼ teaspoon turmeric powder*
- *salt to taste*
- *juice of 1 lime*

## Cooking Instructions

**1.** Bring water to boil in a medium pot. Add potato pieces and boil for 5 minutes, drain, and set aside.

**2.** Heat oil in pan. Sauté onions and curry leaves until onions are translucent.

**3.** Add potatoes, red chilies, Maldive fish, turmeric powder, and salt. Stir-fry for several minutes.

**4.** Squeeze lime juice over before serving.

**Makes 4 to 6 servings**

# Mushroom Curry *(Hathu Curry)*

*While mushrooms might not be popular in Sri Lanka, this dish should not be missed because cooked mushrooms soak up a lot of the curry flavor.*

## Ingredients

- 2 pounds (1 kg) fresh mushrooms
- 2 tablespoons oil
- 1 onion, chopped
- 3 cloves garlic, sliced
- 2 to 3 green chilies, sliced
- 1 sprig curry leaves
- 1 teaspoon black mustard seeds
- 1 tablespoon raw curry powder (page 41)
- 1 teaspoon coriander powder
- 1 teaspoon cayenne pepper powder
- 1/4 teaspoon turmeric powder
- 2 medium tomatoes, blanched and diced
- 1/2 cup (125 ml) coconut milk
- salt to taste

## Cooking Instructions

**1.** Wash mushrooms well and cut into chunky slices.

**2.** Heat oil in pan. Sauté onions, garlic, green chilies, and curry leaves until onions are translucent. Add mustard seeds and fry for 1 to 2 minutes until they start to pop.

**3.** Add mushrooms and all other ingredients. Bring to a boil, then reduce heat and simmer 10 to 15 minutes.

**Makes 4 to 6 servings**

# Cabbage Curry *(Gova Curry)*

*This dish provides a quick and easy accompaniment to rice, and may be made without the addition of coconut milk.*

## Ingredients

- 1 head cabbage
- 1 onion, sliced
- 2 to 3 green chilies, sliced
- 1 tablespoon raw curry powder (page 41)
- 1 teaspoon cayenne pepper powder
- 1/4 teaspoon turmeric powder
- 1/2 cup (125 ml) water
- 1/2 cup (125 ml) coconut milk (optional)
- salt to taste

### For tempering:

- 2 tablespoons oil
- 1 onion, sliced
- 1 sprig curry leaves
- 1/2 teaspoon black mustard seeds
- 1 teaspoon raw curry powder (page 41)

## Cooking Instructions

**1.** Wash cabbage and shred, removing core.

**2.** Combine all ingredients (except ones for tempering) in a pan and cook until cabbage is tender, about 10 to 15 minutes.

**3.** For tempering, heat oil in a pan. Sauté onions and curry leaves until onions are translucent. Add mustard seeds and curry powder and fry another minute. Pour over cabbage and mix well.

Makes 4 to 6 servings

# Sautéed Leeks *(Leeks Temperadu)*

*Leeks have an amazing flavor, but must be cleaned thoroughly in order to remove all the grit that gets lodged in between their layers. For an added twist, thinly sliced potatoes go really well with this dish.*

## Ingredients

- *1 pound (454 g) leeks*
- *2 tablespoons oil or ghee*
- *1 onion, chopped*
- *2 cloves garlic*
- *2-inch (5-cm) piece ginger, chopped*
- *2 to 3 green chilies, sliced*
- *1 sprig curry leaves*
- *½ teaspoon red pepper flakes*
- *1 tomato, blanched and diced*
- *1 tablespoon raw curry powder (page 41)*
- *¼ teaspoon turmeric powder*
- *1 teaspoon salt*

## Cooking Instructions

**1.** Wash and clean leeks and thinly slice.

**2.** Heat oil in pan. Fry onions, garlic, ginger, green chilies, curry leaves, and red pepper flakes until onions are translucent.

**3.** Add leeks, tomato, curry powder, turmeric powder, and salt. Stir-fry on low heat for 5 to 7 minutes until leeks soften.

**Makes 4 to 6 servings**

# Garlic Curry *(Sudulunu Curry)*

*Slow cooking the garlic mellows out its usually strong odor and flavor, while the tamarind adds a tangy note that complements this dish perfectly. The addition of saffron also lends a special flavor—not to mention the fact that garlic is really good for you.*

## Ingredients

- 4 heads garlic
- 5 or 6 small shallots
- 2 tablespoons oil
- 1 sprig curry leaves
- 2 or 3 whole green chilies
- 1 teaspoon fenugreek seeds
- 1 teaspoon cayenne pepper powder
- 1 tablespoon tamarind pulp, soaked in ¼ cup (65 ml) warm water
- pinch of saffron
- 1 cup (250 ml) coconut milk
- salt to taste

## Cooking Instructions

1. Separate garlic cloves. Remove skin from garlic cloves and shallots but keep whole.

2. Heat oil in pan. Fry garlic, shallots, curry leaves, and green chilies for a few minutes. Remove and set aside.

3. Fry fenugreek seeds in hot oil for 2 minutes. Remove.

4. Add all other ingredients to pan and bring to boil. Add fried ingredients, reduce heat and simmer until gravy thickens.

**Makes 4 to 6 servings**

# Chickpea Curry *(Kadalai Curry)*

*This dish of South Indian origin comes from the north of Sri Lanka, home to a predominantly Tamil population. One of the ingredients is garam masala, a popular Indian spice mixture that is readily available at most supermarkets in the U.S. today.*

## Ingredients

- 1 potato, peeled and diced
- 1 (15-ounce) can chickpeas, drained
- ½ cup (125 ml) water
- 1-inch (2.5-cm) piece ginger
- 2 cloves garlic
- ¼ teaspoon turmeric powder
- 2 tablespoons oil
- 1 onion, chopped
- 1 sprig curry leaves
- 1 teaspoon Jaffna curry powder (page 42)
- 1 tomato, blanched and diced
- salt to taste
- 1 teaspoon garam masala
- juice of 1 lemon

## Cooking Instructions

**1.** Boil potato in salted water for 5 minutes.

**2.** Grind ¼ cup of the chickpeas, water, ginger, garlic, and turmeric in food processor or blender.

**3.** Heat oil in pan. Sauté onions and curry leaves until onions are translucent. Add curry powder and mix for 1 minute. Add remaining chickpeas, potato, chickpea puree, tomato, and salt. Stir well and simmer until mixture is thick and creamy.

**4.** Sprinkle with garam masala and lemon juice before serving.

**Makes 4 to 6 servings**

# Soya Curry

*Just to prove that anything can be curried, this newer recipe incorporates dried soya chunks (sometimes known as textured vegetable protein or TVP) that have become popular recently as a healthy alternative to meat.*

## Ingredients

- *12 ounces (340 g) dried soya chunks*
- *2 teaspoons raw curry powder (page 41)*
- *1 to 2 teaspoons cayenne pepper powder*
- *3 cloves garlic, minced*
- *2 teaspoons sliced ginger*
- *2 tablespoons oil*
- *1 onion, sliced*
- *2 to 3 green chilies, sliced*
- *1-inch (2.5-cm) piece pandanus (optional)*
- *1 sprig curry leaves*
- *1 teaspoon tamarind pulp (soaked in ¼ cup warm water, seeds and fiber removed)*
- *1 cup (250 ml) coconut milk*
- *salt to taste*

## Cooking Instructions

**1.** Soak soya chunks in a bowl of boiling water for 10 minutes. Drain and squeeze out water.

**2.** Add curry powder and cayenne powder to soya cubes.

**3.** Grind garlic and ginger together.

**4.** Heat oil in pan. Sauté garlic-ginger paste, onions, green chilies, pandanus, and curry leaves until onions are translucent.

**5.** Add soya chunks and stir-fry for 2 to 3 minutes.

**6.** Mix tamarind with coconut milk and add to pan. Add salt to taste. Cook an additional 5 minutes until gravy reduces and thickens.

---

**Makes 4 to 6 servings**

# Pineapple Curry

*I bet you thought it couldn't be done, but that's why the Sri Lankans had to do it—curry a pineapple. This tasty dish is actually bursting with flavors—sweet, spicy, and sour.*

## Ingredients

- *1 unripe pineapple*
- *1 onion, sliced*
- *2 green chilies, sliced*
- *1-inch (2.5-cm) cinnamon stick*
- *1 teaspoon coriander powder*
- *1 teaspoon cumin powder*
- *2 teaspoons cayenne pepper powder*
- *1½ teaspoons ground dry mustard*
- *½ cup (125 ml) coconut milk*
- *1 teaspoon salt*

**Makes 4 to 6 servings**

## Cooking Instructions

1. Peel and cut pineapple into 1-inch pieces.
2. Mix all ingredients together in a small pot. Bring to a boil and simmer until pineapple has softened, about 20 minutes.

# Mango Curry *(Amba Curry)*

*This sweet/spicy combination once again proves that Sri Lankans will curry anything. The unripe mangoes, coconut milk, and spices add up to a unique dish loaded with flavor. This dish is very popular in the rural south of Sri Lanka where a lot of mangoes grow. When choosing mangoes for this dish make sure they are greenish and still firm.*

## Ingredients

- 2 firm half-ripe mangoes
- 2 tablespoons oil
- 1 onion, sliced
- 3 cloves garlic, chopped
- 2-inch (5-cm) piece ginger, chopped
- 5 dry red chilies, chopped
- 2-inch (5-cm) piece pandanus (optional)
- 1-inch (2.5-cm) cinnamon stick
- 2-inch (5-cm) stalk lemongrass
- 1 sprig curry leaves
- 1 teaspoon black mustard seeds
- 1 tablespoon vinegar
- 1 tablespoon sugar
- 1/4 teaspoon turmeric powder
- 3 cloves
- 1 cup (250 ml) water
- 1 to 2 teaspoons cayenne pepper powder
- 2 tablespoons raw curry powder (page 41)
- 1/2 cup (125 ml) coconut milk
- salt to taste

## Cooking Instructions

**1.** Wash and peel mango and cut into chunks. Prick chunks with fork and cover with salted water and soak for 30 minutes. Drain.

**2.** Heat oil in pan. Sauté onions, garlic, ginger, chilies, pandanus, cinnamon stick, lemongrass, and curry leaves until onions are translucent. Add mustard seeds and sauté for a minute more.

**3.** Add mango, vinegar, sugar, turmeric, cloves, and water and bring to a boil. Reduce heat and simmer for 10 to 15 minutes.

**4.** In another pan, roast cayenne powder and curry powder until fragrant. Mix with coconut milk.

**5.** Add cocunut milk mixture to mango, stir gently and add salt to taste. Cook for 5 more minutes until all flavors are incorporated.

> **Makes 4 to 6 servings**

# Yellow Pumpkin Curry *(Vattakka Curry)*

*Though the pumpkins are slightly different in Sri Lanka, I think any type of pumpkin, or even a butternut squash, would work for this dish.*

## Ingredients

- *1 pound (454 g) pumpkin*
- *1 tablespoon shredded desiccated coconut (unsweetened)*
- *½ teaspoon brown mustard seeds*
- *2 cloves garlic*
- *1 teaspoon chopped ginger*
- *2 tablespoons oil*
- *1 onion, chopped*
- *2 or 3 whole green chilies*
- *1 sprig curry leaves*
- *¾ cup (185 ml) coconut milk*
- *¼ teaspoon turmeric powder*
- *1 teaspoon salt*

**Makes 4 to 6 servings**

## Cooking Instructions

1. Wash and cube pumpkin meat into 1-inch pieces.

2. Grind the coconut, brown mustard seeds, garlic, and ginger together in food processor.

3. Heat oil in pan. Sauté onions, green chilies, and curry leaves until onions are translucent.

4. Add pumpkin, ½ cup of the coconut milk, turmeric powder, and salt and bring to a boil. Reduce heat and simmer 10 to 15 minutes, until pumpkin is tender.

5. Add the blended garlic mixture and remaining ¼ cup coconut milk and mix well. Simmer for another 5 minutes until gravy thickens.

# Cauliflower Curry *(Gova Mal Curry)*

*Certainly not native to the island, cauliflower is considered somewhat exotic in Sri Lanka and is served only on special occasions.*

## Ingredients

- *1 head cauliflower*
- *½ pound (226 g) green peas*
- *2 tablespoons oil*
- *1 onion, sliced*
- *2 to 3 green chilies, sliced*
- *1 sprig curry leaves*
- *1 teaspoon black mustard seeds*
- *2 medium tomatoes, blanched, skinned and diced*
- *2 tablespoons raw curry powder (page 41)*
- *1 teaspoon cayenne pepper powder*
- *½ teaspoon turmeric powder*
- *½ cup (125 ml) water*
- *½ cup (125 ml) coconut milk*
- *salt to taste*

**Makes 4 to 6 servings**

## Cooking Instructions

**1.** Wash and cut cauliflower into florets.

**2.** Boil peas in water to cover until tender. Drain and set aside.

**3.** Heat oil in pan. Sauté onions, green chilies, and curry leaves until onion is translucent.

**4.** Add mustard seeds and fry until they pop, about 1 minute.

**5.** Add tomatoes, curry powder, cayenne powder, and turmeric powder and mix well.

**6.** Add cauliflower florets and mix well.

**7.** Add water, coconut milk, and salt and bring to a boil. Reduce heat and simmer until cauliflower is tender, about 10 to 15 minutes.

**8.** Mix in cooked green peas before serving.

# Lotus Root Badun

*The roots of the lotus flower that rise from the beds of ponds or lakes and snake up to the surface are a unique treat eaten all over Asia. Imagine my surprise when I came across fresh lotus roots in the produce department of H Mart, a Korean supermarket chain in the U.S. If you can't find fresh ones, you can certainly buy them canned at any Asian store. In fact, they might be easier to find than Maldive fish, which will only be available at a Sri Lankan store.*

## Ingredients

- *1 pound lotus root*
- *2 to 3 teaspoons Maldive fish flakes (optional)*
- *1/8 teaspoon turmeric powder*
- *1 medium red onion, sliced*
- *2 to 3 green chilies, chopped*
- *1 to 2 teaspoons cayenne pepper powder*
- *1 tablespoon raw curry powder (page 41)*
- *1 cup (250 ml) coconut milk*
- *2 tablespoons vegetable oil*
- *2 cloves garlic, minced*
- *1 sprig curry leaves*
- *1/2 teaspoon mustard seeds*
- *salt to taste*

**Makes 4 to 6 servings**

## Cooking Instructions

**1.** Boil the whole lotus root in salted water until tender, 10 to 15 minutes. Drain, remove skin, and cut into thin slices.

**2.** Place lotus root slices in a medium saucepan with the Maldive fish, turmeric powder, half the onion, the green chilies, half the cayenne powder, the curry powder, and coconut milk. Bring to a boil and then lower heat and simmer for about 15 minutes, stirring occasionally.

**3.** Heat oil in a pan. Add the rest of the onions, the garlic, and curry leaves and sauté until onions are translucent. Add the mustard seeds and fry for 1 minute more.

**4.** Add the tempered ingredients to the lotus root along with the remaining cayenne powder and salt. Mix well and cook for another 2 minutes.

# Sambols, Chutneys, Pickles, & Salads

$T$he condiments on a Sri Lankan table complement the meal by adding a touch of sweetness or acidity or a kiss of heat to round out the total palette of flavors. Typically, meals will cover the whole spectrum of tastes—sweet, sour, salty, bitter, and spicy—and the pickles, chutneys, sambols and salads that Sri Lankans savor are important details not to be missed when serving this food. Sambols and salads utilize fresh, raw ingredients while the ingredients in most chutneys are boiled down for a long time. For best results, store your sambols and chutneys in a glass jar in the fridge. You must use the sambols within 3 to 4 days, but chutneys will keep for several months.

# Sugar Sambol *(Seeni Sambola)*

*This "relish" is a must at the breakfast table on the Sri Lankan New Year as an accompaniment for milk rice (page 69).*

## Ingredients

- 2 tablespoons oil
- 1 pound (454 g) red onions, finely chopped
- 6 cloves garlic, finely chopped
- 2-inch (5-cm) piece ginger, finely chopped
- 1 sprig curry leaves
- 4 cardamom pods
- 4 cloves
- 2-inch (5-cm) cinnamon stick
- 2 teaspoons salt
- 2 teaspoons cayenne pepper powder
- 5 ounces (150 g) Maldive fish, or dried shrimp
- 5 tablespoons (75 g) tamarind pulp, dissolved in ¼ cup (65 ml) coconut milk
- juice of 1 lime
- 2 teaspoons sugar

## Cooking Instructions

1. Heat oil in pan. Fry onions, garlic, ginger, and curry leaves until onions are golden brown.

2. Add all other ingredients except sugar and cook, uncovered, on low heat for 30 to 45 minutes.

3. Add sugar just before taking off heat and mix well. Cool and store in a glass jar in the fridge for up to 4 days.

> **Makes a 1 pound (454 g) jar**

# Chile Sambol *(Katta Sambol)*

*This seriously spicy condiment goes well with practically any Sri Lankan meal. The inclusion of Maldive fish gives it a very unique flavor and a chewy texture.*

## Ingredients

- *10 whole dried red chilies*
- *1 red onion, finely chopped*
- *1 tablespoon Maldive fish*
- *juice of 1 lime*
- *salt to taste*

## Cooking Instructions

**1.** Coarsely grind chilies in a food processor or blender.

**2.** Add onions and Maldive fish and grind to a coarse paste.

**3.** Remove from blender and mix in lime juice and salt to taste. Store in a glass jar in the fridge for up to 4 days.

# Coconut Sambol *(Pol Sambola)*

*Though sometimes known as the poor man's accompaniment to rice, coconut sambol is popular in every household. It goes great with hoppers, string hoppers, and any breads as well.*

## Ingredients

- *1 onion, chopped*
- *1 teaspoon black peppercorns*
- *2 to 3 teaspoons cayenne pepper powder*
- *6 ounces (170 g) shredded coconut (unsweetened)*
- *1 tablespoon Maldive fish or dried shrimp (optional)*
- *salt to taste*
- *juice of 1 lime*

## Cooking Instructions

1. Grind onions and peppercorns together.
2. Mix all ingredients together in a bowl. Adjust flavors to suite your own taste (either more lime, salt, or cayenne pepper powder). Store in a glass jar in the fridge for up to 4 days.

# Onion Chili Sambol *(Lunu Miris)*

*This fiery mix of onion, chilies, and salty, chewy bits of Maldive fish is the perfect complement to hoppers (page 77) or milk rice (page 69).*

## Ingredients

- *1 onion, chopped*
- *4 tablespoons dry red chili flakes*
- *1 tablespoon Maldive fish or dried shrimp*
- *juice of 1 lime*
- *salt to taste*

## Cooking Instructions

Grind all ingredients together in a food processor or blender to make a thick red paste. Adjust flavors to suite your own taste (either more lime, salt, or chili flakes).

# Mint Sambol *(Minchi Sambola)*

*This refreshing sambol is the perfect complement to lamb biryani (page 73).*

## Ingredients

- 2 ounces (56 g) mint leaves
- 3 or 4 cloves garlic
- 2 or 3 peppercorns
- 2 or 3 green chilies
- juice of 1 lime
- pinch of sugar
- salt to taste

## Cooking Instructions

1. Wash and pat dry mint leaves.
2. Grind all ingredients together in a food processor or blender to make a thick green paste. Store in a glass jar in the fridge for up to 4 days.

# Carrot Sambol *(Karat Sambola)*

*This simple sambol adds a lot of color to a plate and is simultaneously cooling and spicy.*

## Ingredients

- 3 medium to large carrots
- 1 onion, finely chopped
- 1 tomato, diced
- 2 to 3 green chilies, sliced
- ½ teaspoon salt
- ½ teaspoon pepper
- 3 tablespoons shredded unsweetened coconut
- juice of 1 lime

## Cooking Instructions

1. Wash, peel and shred carrots.
2. Combine all ingredients together in a bowl and mix well.
3. Store in a glass jar in the fridge for up to 4 days.

# Bitter Gourd Sambol *(Karavila Sambola)*

*Popular in Indian cuisine, the bitter gourd resembles a small, spiny pickle. Its characteristic bitterness is neutralized by deep frying and the addition of lime juice.*

## Ingredients

- *1 pound (454 g) bitter gourd*
- *oil for frying*
- *1 onion, sliced*
- *2 to 3 green chilies, sliced*
- *1 dry red chili, sliced*
- *1 teaspoon salt*
- *juice of 1 lime*

## Cooking Instructions

**1.** Wash bitter gourd and slice into rounds. Soak in salted water for a few minutes. Drain and pat dry.

**2.** Heat oil in pan. Deep fry bitter gourd until golden brown and crispy. Drain.

**3.** In a bowl combine bitter gourd with all other ingredients.

**4.** Store in a glass jar in the fridge for up to 4 days.

# Radish and Tomato Sambol
## (Raabu Thakkali Sambola)

*Another cooling concoction to take the edge off a spicy dish. I use apple cider vinegar but try it with whatever kind you prefer.*

## Ingredients

- *1 pound (454 g) radishes, peeled and thinly sliced*
- *1 onion, sliced*
- *2 to 3 green chilies, sliced*
- *½ teaspoon sugar*
- *½ teaspoon ground black pepper*
- *1 teaspoon salt*
- *1 tablespoon vinegar*
- *3 red tomatoes, sliced*

## Cooking Instructions

**1.** Soak radish slices in cold salted water for 10 minutes.

**2.** Drain radishes and squeeze out excess water.

**3.** Mix all ingredients in a bowl, adding tomatoes last.

**4.** Store in a glass jar in the fridge for up to 4 days.

# Date & Raisin Chutney *(Rataindhi Chutney)*

*This recipe is one of my Aunt Padma's specialties. The sweetness of the dates and raisins mingled with the heat of cayenne and ginger and the acid of the vinegar creates a very complex flavor.*

## Ingredients

- *1 pound (454 g) dates*
- *1 tablespoon chopped ginger*
- *1 tablespoon chopped garlic*
- *1 to 2 teaspoons cayenne pepper powder*
- *1 to 2 teaspoons salt*
- *1 cup (250 ml) vinegar*
- *½ cup (113 g) sugar*
- *2-inch (5-cm) cinnamon stick*
- *4 ounces (113 g) sultanas or raisins*

## Cooking Instructions

1. Pit dates and cut into small pieces.

2. Blend ginger, garlic, cayenne powder, salt, and a little of the vinegar in a food processor or blender.

3. In a small pot, boil vinegar and sugar with cinnamon stick for 5 minutes. Remove cinnamon stick.

4. Add dates and blended mixture and mix well. Simmer until it thickens slightly. (Note: Mixture should be still a little watery, as it will thicken upon cooling.)

5. Add sultanas or raisins before removing from heat.

6. Pour mixture into glass jars and cool. May be stored in the fridge for 1 to 2 months.

# Mango Chutney *(Amba Chutney)*

*Probably everyone's first introduction to chutney is mango, a sweet counterpoint to an overall spicy meal. Choose mangoes that are green and firm when preparing this recipe.*

## Ingredients

- 4 unripe mangoes (about 2 pounds / 1 kg)
- 1 tablespoon chopped ginger
- 1 tablespoon chopped garlic
- 1 to 2 teaspoons cayenne pepper powder
- 1 tablespoon mustard seeds
- ½ to ¾ cup (125 to 185 ml) vinegar
- 2 teaspoons salt
- 1 pound (454 g) sugar

## Cooking Instructions

**1.** Wash and peel mangoes, and cut into small chunks.

**2.** Blend ginger, garlic, cayenne powder, and mustard seeds in food processor or blender.

**3.** In a small pot, boil vinegar, salt, and sugar until sugar dissolves.

**4.** Stir in mangoes and blended mixture. Boil until mango starts to break down, about 45 to 60 minutes.

**5.** Remove from heat and pour directly into glass jars to cool. May be stored in the fridge for 1 to 2 months.

**Unripe green mangoes (left) are used to make mango chutney**

# Pineapple Chutney *(Annasi Chutney)*

*A rarity in Sri Lanka despite its great flavor, pineapple chutney is only served on special occasions.*

## Ingredients

- *1 pound (454 g) fresh pineapple*
- *1 tablespoon chopped ginger*
- *1 tablespoon chopped garlic*
- *1 to 2 teaspoons cayenne pepper powder*
- *1 tablespoon mustard seeds*
- *½ to ¾ cup (125 to 185 ml) vinegar*
- *10 ounces (283 g) sugar*
- *2 teaspoons salt*
- *2-inch (5-cm) cinnamon stick*

## Cooking Instructions

**1.** Cut off rind from pineapple, remove core, and dice fruit.

**2.** Blend ginger, garlic, cayenne powder, and mustard seeds with a little of the vinegar in food processor or blender.

**3.** Boil vinegar, sugar, salt, and cinnamon stick in a medium pot for 5 minutes, until sugar is dissolved. Remove cinnamon stick.

**4.** Add pineapple and blended mixture and simmer on medium heat for 45 to 60 minutes, until it thickens.

**5.** Pour directly into glass jars to cool. May be stored in the fridge for 1 to 2 months.

# Tamarind Chutney *(Siyambala Chutney)*

*The tart fruit of the tamarind tree lends itself well to a chutney. This dark, rich chutney is pungent and sweet.*

## Ingredients

- *1 pound (454 g) tamarind pulp*
- *1 tablespoon chopped ginger*
- *1 tablespoon chopped garlic*
- *1 to 2 teaspoons cayenne pepper powder*
- *1 tablespoon mustard seeds*
- *½ to ¾ cup (125 to 185 ml) vinegar*
- *1 pound (454 g) sugar*
- *2 teaspoons salt*
- *½ pound (226 g) sultanas or raisins*

## Cooking Instructions

**1.** Soak tamarind in a little vinegar and remove seeds and fiber.

**2.** Grind ginger, garlic, cayenne powder, and mustard seeds with a little vinegar in a food processor or blender.

**3.** Boil vinegar, sugar, and salt until sugar is dissolved.

**4.** Add tamarind and blended mixture and simmer for about 45 minutes, until mixture thickens.

**5.** Stir in sultanas or raisins before removing from heat.

**6.** Pour directly into glass jars to cool. May be stored in the fridge for 1 to 2 months.

# Coconut Chutney *(Pol Chutney)*

*Made with fresh coconut, this savory chutney goes especially well with* Ulundu Vadai *(Savory Donuts, page 54), a South Indian specialty popular in Sri Lanka. If fresh coconut is not readily available, the next best thing is the grated, frozen coconut "meat" that you get at Asian stores. Both simple to make and amazingly good, this condiment may be stored in the fridge for several days.*

## Ingredients

- 1 cup (250 ml) shredded fresh coconut
- 3 green chilies, chopped
- 1 teaspoon minced ginger
- 1 tablespoon roasted chickpeas or peanuts
- salt to taste

### For tempering:
- 1 tablespoon vegetable oil
- 4 curry leaves
- 1 whole dried red chili
- 1 teaspoon black mustard seeds
- 1 teaspoon urad dhal
- $1/4$ teaspoon asafetida powder

## Cooking Instructions

**1.** Grind all ingredients (except those for tempering) in a blender or food processor. Add enough hot water to make it into a paste. Transfer paste into a bowl.

**2.** Heat oil in a pan and add curry leaves, chili, mustard seeds, urad dhal, and asafetida. Fry until mustard seeds start popping and turn gray, about 30 seconds.

**3.** Add tempered ingredients to bowl of coconut paste and stir well.

**4.** Place mixture in a glass jar. May be stored in the fridge for 1 to 2 months.

# Mixed Pickle (Acharu)

*Of Malay origin, this is the most commonly served pickle in Sri Lanka and completes any menu.*

## Ingredients

- 20 small shallots or cocktail onions
- 10 green chilies
- ¼ pound (113 g) green papaya (optional)
- 10 green beans
- 2 small carrots
- ¼ pound (113 g) cauliflower
- 1 cup (250 ml) vinegar
- ½ teaspoon salt

### Spice Paste:
- 1 tablespoon chopped ginger
- 1 tablespoon chopped garlic
- 2 tablespoons sugar
- 1 tablespoon mustard seeds
- ¼ teaspoon turmeric powder
- ¼ cup (65 ml) vinegar
- 1 tablespoon salt

## Cooking Instructions

1. Peel shallots and place in salt water. Split green chilies from stem to tip. Peel papaya and cut into small strips. Cut beans and carrots into 1 to 2-inch (2.5 to 5-cm) strips. Separate cauliflower into florets.

2. Bring vinegar with salt to a boil and cook each type of vegetable separately in it for 1 minute each. Drain and set aside in a bowl together.

3. Grind spice paste ingredients in a blender or food processor. Pour over vegetables and mix well.

4. Store in a glass jar in the fridge for 2 to 3 days before using. Will keep for up to 2 months.

# Lime Pickle *(Lunu Dehi)*

*Lime pickle is probably the most popular condiment in Sri Lanka, and almost everyone enjoys a dollop on their plate of rice and curry. Of course, the pungency of this pickle makes it a very acquired taste.*

## Ingredients

- 10 limes
- 2 tablespoons coarse salt
- 3 cups (750 ml) vinegar
- 12 ounces (340 g) sugar

## Cooking Instructions

1. Wash and dry limes. Cut them in half, prick with fork and rub with salt. Leave the limes in a covered pot for 3 days.

2. Sun dry limes for 3 days (covering them at night).

3. Place limes in a glass jar with the vinegar and sugar. Seal and store for 6 months before using. Though limes will turn brown in color, they can be kept indefinitely.

# Tomato Cucumber Salad

*This simple refreshing salad is a must for all rice and curry meals for its cooling effect that complements spicy dishes. For an added twist, add a few slices of hard-boiled egg on top.*

## Ingredients

- 2 medium tomatoes, sliced
- 1 cucumber, sliced
- 1 onion, sliced
- 2 to 3 green chilies, sliced
- 1 teaspoon Maldive fish (optional)
- juice of 1 lime
- salt to taste

## Cooking Instructions

Combine all ingredients in a bowl and mix well. Be careful not to bruise the tomatoes. May be served immediately or kept in the fridge.

# Desserts

*O*ut of all the foreign contributions to Sri Lankan cuisine, desserts seem to be the most prevalent. Caramel pudding (also known as crème caramel or flan) comes from the Portuguese; broeder, a Christmas fruitcake, from the Dutch; puddings of rice, bread, and that fancy concoction known as Christmas pudding from the British; and coconut flan from the Malays. Indian sweets, heavy on the milk and ghee, are also very popular on the island. Of course, there are a wide range of local sweets as well, most made with some form of coconut and jaggery (palm sugar). But Sri Lankans aren't picky. Sometimes a scoop of ice cream and some fruit salad is the perfect ending to a spicy meal.

# Ammi's Love Cake

*This very moist, rich, and fragrant cake is one of my mother's specialties, always made with lots of love. While somewhat labor intensive it does produce a cake like no other, which Sri Lankans usually enjoy with a cup of tea. And, no, the 10 egg yolks that the recipe calls for is not a misprint.*

## Ingredients

- *1 pound (454 g) unsalted cashew nuts*
- *½ pound (226 g) semolina*
- *¼ pound (113 g) butter, cubed*
- *10 egg yolks*
- *1 pound (454 g) sugar*
- *½ cup (125 ml) honey*
- *½ teaspoon rose essence*
- *¼ teaspoon grated nutmeg*
- *¼ teaspoon grated lemon rind*
- *¼ teaspoon ground cinnamon*
- *¼ teaspoon ground allspice*
- *1 tablespoon all-purpose flour*

## Cooking Instructions

**1.** Roast cashews on medium heat. Cool and chop small. Set aside.

**2.** Prepare a 9x12 pan with 4 layers of newspaper and 2 layers of parchment paper to prevent burning the sides and bottom of the cake. Butter parchment paper evenly or use a non-stick spray.

**3.** Preheat oven to 350 degrees F (175 degrees C).

**4.** In a medium saucepan, roast semolina. When warm, add butter. Stir until melted and then cool.

**5.** Beat yolks in a large bowl for 1 minute. Add sugar and beat until creamy.

**6.** Stir in honey, rose essence, nutmeg, lemon rind, cinnamon, and allspice.

**7.** Add chopped cashews. Fold in semolina mixture and flour.

**8.** Pour into prepared pan and bake at 350 degrees F (175 degrees C) for 15 minutes; lower to 325 degrees F (160 degrees C) and bake for an additional 30 minutes or until slightly golden and a toothpick inserted into center comes out clean.

# Caramel Pudding

*This universally loved dessert, known by many names (like flan or crème caramel) and found in many cultures, is so easy to make (and even easier to eat). The Portuguese introduced it to Sri Lanka along with such other indispensable food items as the chili pepper, tomato, and potato.*

## Ingredients

- 2 to 3 tablespoons sugar (for caramel)
- 1 small can (14 oz/396 g) sweetened condensed milk
- 1½ cans water
- 4 eggs, beaten
- few drops vanilla extract

## Cooking Instructions

1. Heat sugar with 1 tablespoon water in a 2-quart stainless steel mold until golden (do not stir). Swirl the melted sugar to coat base and sides.

2. In a bowl mix condensed milk, water, eggs, and vanilla.

3. Pour into prepared mold, cover with tin foil, and steam in a double boiler for 30 minutes until set. (The water should not boil under it but simmer gently.)

4. Remove from heat and allow to cool.

5. Cover and refrigerate for 5 to 6 hours before serving. You can either serve this from the mold or turn the pudding out onto a serving plate.

# Jaggery

The use of unrefined whole cane and palm sugar is common throughout Asia, Africa, Latin America, and the Caribbean. In Sri Lanka, this natural sweetener assumes the form of jaggery, a product derived from the coconut palm. Jaggery starts off as the milky sap extracted from coconut flowers, which quickly ferments into "toddy" or "palm wine." After being boiled with a little salt (for its preservative quality), it becomes a dense, dark brown syrup that is poured into the split halves of coconut shells and cooled, giving it its characteristic shape. Good jaggery has a dark brown color and a soft consistency as opposed to lighter, harder product, which has probably been adulterated with sugar. If the toddy, or fermented sap, is not boiled down into jaggery, it is usually distilled in wooden vats to make Sri Lanka's liquor of choice, Arrack, which comes from the Arabic word for "strong liquor."

Full of minerals not found in ordinary sugar—like calcium and phosphates—and not introduced into the blood stream as rapidly, jaggery's health benefits are recognized within the Ayurvedic system of medicine. It is sometimes prescribed for people with sore throats as well as being used in the treatment of lung infections. But for most Sri Lankans, jaggery is simply the sweetener of choice with a taste most similar to brown sugar (a suitable substitute in most recipes). In villages, people often keep a small chunk of jaggery in their mouth while sipping tea instead of sweetening the beverage directly.

The best quality jaggery comes from the kittul palm (Caryota urens), which is only found in India, Sri Lanka, and Myanmar. The syrup made from kittul jaggery, known as treacle, completes a popular dessert when served over buffalo milk curd (yogurt). ❖

# Shymala's Coconut Custard Pudding (Wattalampan)

*This island favorite, introduced to Sri Lanka by Malay traders, is a thicker, richer version of caramel pudding. It is made with coconut milk and jaggery, a sweetener derived from the sap of the coconut palm flower. My cousin Shymala makes an especially good one.*

## Ingredients

- *8 eggs*
- *¾ pound (340 g) grated jaggery*
- *2 cups (500 ml) thick coconut milk*
- *1 tablespoon corn flour*
- *½ teaspoon grated nutmeg*
- *¼ teaspoon cardamom powder*
- *½ cup (125 ml) chopped cashews*

## Cooking Instructions

1. Beats eggs well in a bowl.

2. Add the other ingredients except cashews and mix well.

3. Strain and pour into a 2½-quart stainless steel mold. Cover with foil and steam in a double boiler for 30 to 40 minutes until set. (The water should not boil under it but simmer gently.)

4. Remove from heat and allow to cool. Cover and refrigerate 5 to 6 hours. Sprinkle with the chopped cashews before serving.

# Leela's Legendary Milk Toffee

*Don't think of this as the hard English toffee or the chewy American kind. Leela, my Aunt Dora's maid of 32 years, makes this sweet dessert—closer to fudge than toffee— that crumbles easily when chewed and melts in your mouth.*

## Ingredients

- *1 large can (525 g) sweetened condensed milk*
- *4 tablespoons sugar*
- *4 tablespoons butter or margarine*
- *few drops vanilla extract*
- *4 tablespoons chopped cashews (optional)*

## Cooking Instructions

**1.** Put condensed milk, sugar, butter, and vanilla extract in a small pan.

**2.** Cook on low heat, stirring constantly, until mixture is thick, about 30 minutes.

**3.** Pour onto a greased board and spread about 1-inch thick. Cut into squares while still hot and then allow to cool. Top with cashews.

# Coconut Rock

*This dessert is like a Mounds candy bar without the chocolate covering—just soft, chewy sweet coconut goodness.*

## Ingredients

- 2 pounds (1 kg) sugar
- 1 cup (250 ml) milk
- 1 pound (454 g) freshly grated or desiccated coconut
- 2 tablespoons chopped cashews
- food coloring (optional)

## Cooking Instructions

**1.** In a small pan, dissolve sugar in milk and bring to a boil.

**2.** Add coconut and cook on medium heat, stirring constantly, until mixture leaves the sides of the pan.

**3.** Add cashews (and food coloring if desired) before removing from heat. Mix well.

**4.** Spread on greased board to about 1-inch thick. Cut into squares while still hot and then cool.

# Rice Pudding

*As the British were Sri Lanka's longest colonial rulers, they had to import some of the comforts of home. This particular comfort food became an instant hit with the rice-loving Sri Lankans.*

## Ingredients

- ¼ pound (113 g) basmati rice
- 3½ cups (875 ml) water
- 1 small can (14 oz/396 g) sweetened condensed milk
- ¼ teaspoon ground cinnamon
- ½ teaspoon cardamom powder
- ¼ cup (65 ml) chopped cashews
- ¼ cup (65 ml) raisins or sultanas

## Cooking Instructions

1. Wash rice and cook with the water for 5 to 10 minutes.

2. Add condensed milk and bring to a boil. Reduce heat and simmer, stirring constantly, until mixture thickens, about 30 to 45 minutes.

3. Add cinnamon and cardamom powder.

4. Remove from heat and pour into a bowl. Cool in fridge for 2 to 3 hours.

5. Garnish with nuts and raisins.

# Bread Pudding

*This easy to prepare dessert was popularized by the British who used stale, leftover bread to make it. My grandfather loved to eat bread pudding with a homemade custard sauce (page 193).*

## Ingredients

- 8 slices of bread (any store-bought pre-sliced white bread would work)
- 2 tablespoons butter
- ¼ cup (65 ml) raisins
- ½ small can (from a 14 oz/396 g can) sweetened condensed milk
- 1 cup (250 ml) milk
- 2 beaten eggs
- pinch of ground allspice

## Cooking Instructions

1. Heat oven to 300 degrees F (150 degrees C). Remove bread crusts and butter both sides of each slice. Cut into triangles and arrange in an ovenproof pan (7x9 inch). Sprinkle raisins in between slices.

2. In a bowl, combine condensed milk, milk, eggs, and allspice and beat well. Pour mixture over bread slices and allow to sit a few minutes for absorption.

3. Bake for 30 to 40 minutes until the top is golden brown. May be served hot or cold.

# Paradise Isle Fruit Salad

*Nothing soothes the soul more than a light and cool dessert to help digest a heavy meal. For an added boost serve with custard (page 193) or ice cream.*

## Ingredients

- *1 small pineapple*
- *1 small papaya*
- *2 mangoes*
- *2 bananas*
- *1 tablespoon lemon juice*
- *1 tablespoon sugar*
- *¼ cup (65 ml) shredded sweetened coconut*

## Cooking Instructions

**1.** Peel all fruits and cut into bite-size chunks. Combine in a bowl and sprinkle with lemon juice and sugar.

**2.** Cover with plastic wrap and place in fridge for 2 hours to chill.

**3.** Garnish with shredded coconut.

# Custard

*No fruit salad, bread pudding, or Christmas pudding is complete without this delicious topping. In fact, try it on apple pie or even a bowl of fresh strawberries.*

## Ingredients

- *1 can (14 oz/396 g) sweetened condensed milk*
- *4 egg yolks*
- *¼ cup (65 ml) sugar*
- *¼ teaspoon grated nutmeg*
- *pinch of ground allspice*
- *1 teaspoon vanilla extract*

## Cooking Instructions

**1.** Pour condensed milk into a saucepan along with one can of water.

**2.** Beat the egg yolks. Add to milk mixture along with the sugar, nutmeg, and allspice and stir well with wooden spoon over low heat. Continue stirring to avoid lumps.

**3.** When the spoon is thinly coated with custard, remove from heat and keep stirring until cool.

**4.** Add vanilla and put in fridge to chill.

# Tea

Known far and wide, Ceylon tea has consistently been one of Sri Lanka's biggest exports, keeping pace in the international market even among such top producers as China and India. Today it stakes its claim as the only single origin tea in the world (as opposed to standard supermarket multi-origin teas, which are a blend of leaves from thirty or more countries) as well as the only tea still plucked by hand and minimally processed.

Introduced in 1867 by British planter James Taylor, tea quickly replaced coffee as the thriving cash crop on Sri Lanka following the scourge of *Hemileia Vastatrix* (or Coffee Rust), a fungal disease that afflicted most of Sri Lanka's coffee plantations. Taylor's first cuttings, taken from Assam, India, took root at Loolecondra Estate in Kandy in the island's central highlands, where the low humidity, cool temperatures, and adequate rainfall provided the ideal climate for the crop. Between 1873 and 1880, tea production rose from just 23 pounds to 81.3 tons a year. By 1890 that number had reached 22,900 tons. Advancements in technology accompanied the steady rise of tea production so that by 1927 Sri Lanka was exporting over 100,000 metric tons of tea a year. That number doubled by 1965 ,making Sri Lanka the world's largest tea exporter.

Driving this production was a workforce of Indian Tamils (mostly women, whose smaller hands were considered better-suited for the task of plucking leaves from the short bushes) initially imported by the British to work the coffee plantations. Developing their own community distinct from Sri Lankan Tamils, these Indian Tamils, according to recent estimates, number around 300,000 today. If you take a trip to Sri Lanka's highlands you can see them dotting the teeming green slopes in brightly colored saris, filling the huge woven baskets on their backs with speed, grace, precision, and lots of tea leaves.

After being gathered, the bales of tea are brought to musk sheds, where they are weighed and undergo an initial inspection. From there the leaves proceed to an on-site factory where they are withered by large blowers. Then they are cut to release their juices, a key step that commences the fermentation process. Finally, the leaves are fired to lock in the flavor and dried.

In order for a tea to be marked "Pure Ceylon Tea—Packed In Sri Lanka" it undergoes a rigorous inspection by the Sri Lanka Tea Board. Of the three grades of Sri Lankan tea—ranked according to elevation grown—High or Up-country (*Udarata*), characterized by its golden hue and intense flavor, is considered the best followed by Mid-country (*Medarata*), and Low country. The latter, though lacking the distinctive flavor of higher grown teas, is still of good quality. There are further gradings based on size and appearance—namely "Leaf" grades, such as Orange Pekoe (OP) and "Broken" grades such as Broken Orange Pekoe Fannings (BOPF).

But, of course, you need know nothing about this process to enjoy a nice cup of Sri Lanka's most popular export. Most Ceylon tea—about 70% to be exact—goes to former Soviet block countries, The Middle East, and North Africa—but the British are still big fans as are the Japanese. Tea, which originated in China, has become a universal beverage, enjoyed in many different ways. In Sri Lanka they still brew a cup that would make the British proud. ✦

## How to Make a Cup of Tea

In Sri Lanka, tea is consumed at any time of the day—not just during the traditional afternoon tea time.

*1.* Add one teaspoon of loose tea leaves per person to a warm teapot.

*2.* Top up with boiling water. Allow to infuse for a minute or two.

*3.* Stir, then allow leaves to settle.

*4.* Pour through a fine strainer.

*5.* Add milk/sugar to taste.

# Christmas Pudding

*One of the more lasting contributions by the British, Christmas pudding is among the richest desserts on the planet. Though we are Buddhist Sinhalese, my family still celebrates Christmas, and the season would not be complete without this dessert. As a child, I used to love how it was doused with cognac and brought flaming to the table to eat with either brandy sauce or custard.*

## Ingredients

- 2 cups (500 ml) brown raisins
- 2 cups (500 ml) white/golden raisins
- 1 cup (250 ml) currants
- 1 cup (250 ml) finely chopped candied fruit mix
- 1 cup (250 ml) finely chopped candied cherries
- 1 apple, peeled and grated
- 1 carrot, grated
- 1 cup (250 ml) chopped unsalted cashews
- 1 tablespoon finely grated lemon peel
- 1 tablespoon finely grated orange peel
- juice of 1 lemon
- juice of 1 orange
- 1 teaspoon cardamom powder, roasted
- 1 teaspoon ground cloves, roasted
- 1 teaspoon grated nutmeg
- 1 cup (250 ml) sherry
- 1 cup (250 ml) brandy
- 1 cup (250 ml) butter
- 1 cup (250 ml) packed brown sugar
- 6 eggs
- 4 cups (1 liter) fresh breadcrumbs
- 2 cups (500 ml) flour

## Cooking Instructions

**1.** In a deep bowl, combine the fruits, carrot, nuts, peels, juices, spices, sherry, and brandy. Cover tightly and leave overnight.

**2.** On the following day, cream the butter and sugar together. Add eggs and beat well. Fold into fruit mixture.

**3.** Fold in the breadcrumbs in parts alternating with the flour.

**4.** Fill medium stainless steel pudding bowls with mixture (2 inches from top) and cover each with 2 layers of parchment paper. Tie string around bowls so they are watertight. Cover with tin foil to further seal.

**5.** Place bowls in saucepans filled with hot water that comes a quarter of the way up the bowl.

**6.** Steam puddings for 4 hours keeping water at a low boil and making sure that there is always enough water in the pans to cook them but not boil over.

**7.** Remove from heat and cool.

**8.** Remove original paper and re-cover with fresh parchment. Seal with foil. The pudding can be stored in a cool place for up to 6 months.

**9.** On Christmas day, steam pudding for a further 2 hours and serve hot with custard (page 193) or brandy sauce.

# Aunty Sita's Chocolate Biscuit Pudding

*This scrumptious dessert recalls the joys of dunking cookies into milk as a child. It requires no cooking, and qualifies as a contemporary Sri Lankan favorite. My Aunt Sita makes an incredibly wicked one.*

## Ingredients

- *1 pound (454 g) confectioner's sugar*
- *1 pound (454 g) cocoa powder*
- *1 pound (454 g) unsalted butter, softened*
- *2 teaspoons vanilla extract*
- *splash of brandy (optional)*
- *30 to 40 chocolate cookies*
- *1 cup (250 ml) milk*
- *½ pound (226 g) roasted unsalted cashews, chopped*

## Cooking Instructions

1. Beat sugar, cocoa powder, butter, and vanilla together in a bowl to a creamy consistency, adding a splash of brandy if you like.

2. Rub another large bowl with some butter.

3. Dip cookies in milk and place some in a single layer in the bowl.

4. Place a generous spoonful of the cocoa mixture on top, spreading it out evenly.

5. Place a layer of chopped cashews on top of this. Repeat layering until all ingredients are used.

6. Set in fridge for 2 to 3 hours before serving.

# Baked Sago Pudding

*Sago is a seed that gets somewhat swelled and gelatinous when wet, like tapioca.*

## Ingredients

- *½ small can (from a 14 oz/396 g can) sweetened condensed milk*
- *2 cups (500 ml) water*
- *4 heaping tablespoons sago*
- *pinch of salt*
- *2 or 3 eggs, separated*
- *dash of lemon juice*

## Cooking Instructions

1. Heat oven to 350 degrees F (175 degrees C).

2. Combine condensed milk, water, and sago in a medium pan and bring to a boil. Reduce heat and simmer until thick, about 30 to 45 minutes.

3. Mix in salt. Remove from heat.

4. Add well-beaten egg yolks and lemon juice. Beat egg whites to stiff peaks. Fold the beaten egg whites into the batter.

5. Pour mixture into a greased pie dish and bake for about 1 hour, until pudding is browned and set.

# Rasawalli Pudding *(King Yam Pudding)*

*This Jaffna specialty is a quick, easy, and healthy dessert. You also may use regular yams or sweet potatoes.*

## Ingredients

- *1 pound (454 g) rasawalli yams*
- *2 cups (500 ml) coconut milk*
- *1 cup (250 ml) coconut cream*
- *4 ounces (113 g) sugar*
- *salt to taste*

## Cooking Instructions

1. Wash, peel, and cut yams into thin slices.

2. Cook yam slices in a pan with coconut milk until soft.

3. Remove from heat and mash the yams with the back of a wooden spoon. Add coconut cream and sugar and bring to a boil. Cook until all sugar has dissolved. Add salt to taste.

4. Serve pudding hot or cold.

# Coconut Sweetmeat *(Kalu Dodol)*

*This local specialty, somewhat akin to a coconut fudge, takes patience and a lot of stamina (stirring), but your effort is rewarded with a chewy and delicious sweet.*

## Ingredients

- 1 pound (454 g) jaggery (palm sugar)
- 3 ounces (85 g) cashew nuts, chopped
- 6 cups (1.5 liters) coconut milk
- ½ teaspoon cardamom powder
- 4 ounces (113 g) rice flour
- 2 ounces (56 g) cashews (for garnish)

## Cooking Instructions

1. Scrape the jaggery into small pieces.

2. Place jaggery in a large bowl with cashews. Add the coconut milk and cardamom powder. Gradually mix in the flour so that there are no lumps.

3. Pour mixture into a saucepan and cook over medium-high heat, stirring constantly, until it thickens. As the mixture forms into a mass, oil will begin to form around the sides. Remove oil with a metal spoon.

4. Pour the mixture into an 8 x 10 baking pan and allow it to cool.

5. Garnish with cashews. Cut into pieces and serve.

# Sample Menus

In Sri Lanka, rice and curry are served all together, buffet-style, so diners may pick and choose from a variety of meat, fish, and vegetable dishes. There is also usually at least one chutney or pickle, a fresh salad, and papadum (crispy, wafer-thin chips made from lentil flour that are deep-fried, available at any Indian store). When putting together a menu, attention should be paid to the interplay of the colors, textures, and flavors that will ultimately be presented and eaten together. Pay extra attention to the amount of chili/cayenne powder you use when preparing the curries so as not to lose any guests along the way, and be sure to include mild dishes along with the spicy ones.

## Menus for 4 to 6 people

- Basic Rice (page 66)
- Chicken Curry (page 87) or
  Shrimp Curry (page 115)
- Sri Lankan Lentils (page 125)
- Mallun (page 135)
- Eggplant Curry (page 143)
- Coconut Sambol (page 163)

---

- Ghee Rice (page 70)
- Beef Curry (page 91) or
  Red Fish Curry (page 117)
- Spiced Potatoes (page 147)
- Moong Bean Curry (page 140)
- Okra Curry (page 145)
- Onion Chili Sambol (page 164)

---

**Vegetarian**
- Yellow Rice (page 67)
- French Bean Curry (page 137)
- Carrot Curry (page 131)
- Chickpea Curry (page 152)
- Tomato Cucumber Salad (page 177)
- Bitter Gourd Sambol (page 167)

## Menus for 6 to 8 people

- Basic Rice (page 66)
- Lamb Curry (page 92) or
  Pork Curry (page 89)
- Crab Curry (page 111) or
  Squid Curry (page 103)
- Cabbage Curry (page 149)
- Potato Curry (page 132)
- Mallun (page 135)
- Carrot Sambol (page 166)

---

- Yellow Rice (page 67)
- Sour Fish Curry (page 121)
- Liver, Peas & Cashew Curry (page 94)
- Sri Lankan Lentils (page 125)
- Sautéed Leeks (page 150)
- Radish & Tomato Sambol (page 168)

---

### Vegetarian
- Vegetable Fried Rice (page 71)
- Soya Curry (page 153)
- Yellow Pumpkin Curry (page 156)
- Mushroom Curry (page 148)
- Spinach Curry (page 133)
- Beet Curry (page 131)
- Tomato Cucumber Salad (page 177)

## Menus for 8 to 10 people

- Basic Rice (page 66)
- Chicken Curry (page 87) or
  Pork Curry (page 89)
- Beef Curry (page 91) or
  Lamb Curry (page 92)
- Deviled Shrimp (page 113) or
  Deviled Squid (page 113)
- Sri Lankan Lentils (page 125)
- French Bean Curry (page 137)
- Mallun (page 135)
- Fish Cutlets (page 51)
- Coconut Sambol (page 163)

---

- Yellow Rice (page 67) or
  Ghee Rice (page 70)
- Fish Mustard Curry (page 119) or
  Shrimp Curry (page 115)
- Mutton Curry (page 92) or
  Deviled Beef (page 95)
- Mushroom Curry (page 148)
- Eggplant Curry (page 143)
- Cauliflower Curry (page 157)
- Mango Curry (page 155)
- Carrot Sambol (page 166)

---

# Resources

**Online sites for Sri Lankan products:**

www.lankadelight.com
www.lankaspice.com
www.lakfood.com

**Skiz's Original Spice Blends:**

www.foodoro.com
www.foodzie.com

# Index

# About the Author

**S.H. ("Skiz") Fernando Jr.** is a second generation Sri Lankan-American and graduate of Harvard University and the Columbia University School of Journalism. As a music journalist, he has written for *The New York Times, Rolling Stone, Vibe,* and *Spin.* He is the author of *The New Beats: Exploring the Music, Culture & Attitudes of Hip-Hop* (Anchor/Doubleday). He's produced several albums on his WordSound label, and is also writer/ director of several films. In 2006, he moved to Sri Lanka for a year to learn about its cuisine and research this cookbook. In March 2009, he was featured on Travel Channel's *No Reservations with Anthony Bourdain,* where he led the crew to Sri Lanka's hot spots.

Skiz blogs about Sri Lankan food and all things spicy at *www. riceandcurry.wordpress.com* and will be happy to answer any of your queries about Sri Lankan food. He also makes his own brand of curry powder, Skiz's Original Sri Lankan Curry Powder (raw and roasted), which is available at *www.foodoro.com* and *www.foodzie.com.* He resides in Baltimore, M.D. ✤

# Also available from Hippocrene Books . . .

## HEALTHY SOUTH INDIAN COOKING
### Expanded Edition
*Alamelu Vairavan and Dr. Patricia Marquardt*

With the addition of fifty new easy-to-prepare dishes, *Healthy South Indian Cooking* is back, now totaling 250 recipes. In the famous **Chettinad** cooking tradition of southern India, these mostly vegetarian recipes allow home cooks to create dishes such as Potato-filled **Dosas** with Coconut Chutney; Pearl Onion and Tomato **Sambhar;** Chickpea and Bell Pepper **Poriyal;** and Eggplant Masala Curry. **Rasams**, breads, legumes and **payasams** are all featured here, as is the exceptional **Chettinad** Chicken **Kolambu,** South India's version of the popular **vindaloo.** Each of these low-fat, low-calorie recipes come with a complete nutritional analysis. Also included are sample menus and innovative suggestions for integrating South Indian dishes into traditional Western meals. A section on the varieties and methods of preparation for **dals** (a lentil dish that is a staple of this cuisine), a multilingual glossary of spices and ingredients, and 16 pages of color photographs make this book a clear and concise introduction to the healthy, delicious cooking of South India.
ISBN: 0-7818-1189-9 · $35.00hc

## THE KERALA KITCHEN
### Recipes and Recollections from the Syrian Christians of South India
*Lathika George*

Since ancient times, seafarers and traders have been drawn by the lure of spices to Kerala, a verdant, tropical state on the Malabar Coast of South India. It is this legacy that *The Kerala Kitchen* brings us, through 150 delectable recipes and the unforgettable stories that accompany them. Featured here are such savory delights as **Meen Vevichathu** – fish curry cooked in a clay pot, **Parippu** – lentils with coconut milk, and **Thiyal** – shallots with tamarind and roasted coconut. Equally mouthwatering are an array of rice preparations and tempting desserts. Authentic and easy to prepare, these recipes are adapted for the western kitchen, and accompanied by a guide to spices, herbs, and equipment, as well as a glossary of food terms. Interwoven between these recipes, in the best tradition of the cookbook memoir, are tales of talking doves, toddy shops, traveling chefs, and killer coconuts. Full of beautiful photographs, charming illustrations, and lyrical memories of food and family.
ISBN: 978-0-7818-1184-2 · $35.00hc

## FLAVORFUL INDIA
**Treasured Recipes from a Gujarati Family**
*Priti **Chitnis** Gress*

Located in northwestern India, Gujarat is known as the country's "Garden State," and is renowned for its vegetarian specialties. *Flavorful India* showcases the cuisine of Gujarat—from street foods like crunchy snack mix and vegetable fritters, to traditional home-cooked dishes that feature an abundance of locally available vegetables like okra, eggplant, bottle gourd, and many **varieties** of beans. Spicy ***dals***, delicate flatbreads, and traditional sweets and beverages bring the Gujarati dining experience full circle. A chapter on the meat, poultry, and fish specialties that are enjoyed in the region is also included. This collection of authentic family recipes will introduce you to some of India's most delicious, yet often overlooked, culinary offerings. An introduction to Gujarati culture, sections on spices, ingredients, and utensils, and charming line drawings by the author's father bring the flavors of India to life.
ISBN: 0-7818-1207-0 · $14.95pb


## MENUS AND MEMORIES FROM PUNJAB
**Meals to Nourish Body and Soul**
*Veronica "Rani" Sidhu*

"Sidhu has dipped into—and helped preserve—a rich culinary tradition that extends back hundreds of years."
—Andrew F. Smith, food historian and editor-in-chief of *The Oxford Encyclopedia of Food and Drink in America*

Arranged in a unique format of 22 full menus, this cookbook takes readers on a nostalgic culinary journey through Punjab. Featured are 146 recipes from signature village fare like Buttermilk Stew with Vegetable ***Pakoras*** to a stunning Roast Leg of Lamb that has graced the tables of Maharajahs. A colorful historical vignette or family anecdote introduces each menu, bringing the culture and cuisine of Punjab alive for readers. Also included are 16 pages of beautiful color photographs, glossaries of food and religious terms, and a resource guide for finding Indian ingredients.
ISBN: 978-0-7818-1220-7 · $29.95hc

## TASTE OF NEPAL
*Jyoti Pandey Pathak*

Winner of "Best Foreign Cuisine Book" at the 2008 Gourmand World Cookbook Awards, *Taste of Nepal* is a thorough and comprehensive guide to this cuisine. One of very few Nepali cookbooks available, this book features more than 350 authentic recipes, plus sections on Nepali herbs and spices, menu planning, Nepalese kitchen equipment, and delightful illustrations. There is something for everyone in this book—for the most timid cook Fried Rice **(Baasi-Bhaat Bhutuwa)** or Stir-Fried Chicken **(Kukhura Taareko)** are easily achievable, but the adventurous will be tempted to try Goat Curry **(Khasi-Boka ko Maasu)** and Sun-Dried Fish with Tomato Chutney **(Golbheda ra Sidra Maacha).**
ISBN: 0-7818-1121-X · $27.50 hc

## CUISINES OF PORTUGUESE ENCOUNTERS
**Expanded Edition**
*Cherie Hamilton*

"What a joy to have access to the marvelous foods generated by Portugal's fifteenth and sixteenth century explosion into the worlds of Asia, Africa, the Americas, and the Southern oceans . . . a great story!"
—Nahum Waxman, Owner of Kitchen Arts and Letters, NYC

Now expanded to over 300 authentic recipes, **this cookbook encompass** the entire Portuguese-speaking world. Menus for religious holidays and festive occasions, a glossary, a section on mail-order sources, a brief history of the cuisines, a section of color photographs, and a bilingual index assist the home chef in creating meals that celebrate the rich, diverse, and delicious culinary legacy of this old empire.
ISBN: 978-0-7818-1181-1 • $29.95hc

# FLAVORS OF MALAYSIA
## A Journey through Time, Tastes, and Traditions
*Susheela Raghavan*

*Flavors of Malaysia* celebrates the best of the Malaysian table: sizzling **satays**, flavorful stir-fries, fragrant rice and noodle dishes, aromatic curries, and Malaysia's signature hot and spicy condiments, the delectable **sambals.**

For centuries Malaysia was a major center of the spice trade in Southeast Asia. Over time, Malay, Chinese, Indian, Thai, Indonesian and Arab, as well as Dutch, Portuguese, and British influences blended beautifully to create the mélange of cultures and intensely vibrant flavors that is Malaysian cuisine today.

Susheela Raghavan serves up treasured recipes, touching family stories, and fascinating notes about the origins of Malaysian food in this lovingly compiled collection.
ISBN: 978-0-7818-1249-8 • $40.00hc

Prices subject to change without prior notice. **To purchase Hippocrene Books** contact your local bookstore, visit www.hippocrenebooks.com, call (212) 685-4373, or write to: HIPPOCRENE BOOKS, 171 Madison Avenue, New York, NY 10016.

WARREN TWP LIBRARY
42 MOUNTAIN BLVD

JAN 2 6 2012

WARREN, NJ 07059
908-754-5554